Breakfast & Brunch Dishes

Recent Titles in
Foodservice Menu Planning Series

Volume Feeding Menu Selector by Alta B. Atkinson
Eulalia C. Blair, Editor

Luncheon and Supper Dishes
Eulalia C. Blair

Salads and Salad Dressings
Eulalia C. Blair

Breakfast & Brunch Dishes

FOR FOODSERVICE MENU PLANNING

Selected by

EULALIA C. BLAIR

Jule Wilkinson, Editor

CAHNERS BOOKS

A Division of Cahners Publishing Company, Inc.
89 Franklin St., Boston, Massachusetts 02110
Publishers of Institutions/VF Magazine

Library of Congress Cataloging in Publication Data

Blair, Eulalia C   comp.
  Breakfast and brunch dishes for foodservice menu planning.

  1. Breakfasts. 2. Brunches. 3. Cookery for institutions, etc. I. Title.
TX733.B6   641.5'72   74-34100
ISBN 0-8436-2057-9

Copyright © 1975 by Cahners Publishing Company, Inc.
All rights reserved. This book or parts of it may not be reproduced in any form without permission of the publisher.

ISBN 0-8436-2057-9
Printed in the United States of America

TABLE OF CONTENTS

INTRODUCTION	1
BREAKFAST	3
FRUITS, JUICES, BEVERAGES	7
CEREALS	19
MEAT, CHICKEN AND FISH	27
PANCAKES	53
WAFFLES	65
FRITTERS	71
FRENCH TOAST	77
SYRUPS	84
EGG DISHES	91
OMELETS	105
SHORTCAKES AND BENEDICT	114
POTATO DISHES	117
BREADS	123
Muffins	125
Corn Breads	149
Coffee Cakes	154

Quick Loaf Breads	171
Biscuits and Sweet Rolls from Biscuit Dough	177
Yeast Rolls	183
Kuchens	195
Doughnuts	201
Scones, Gingerbread, Popovers, Sally Lunn	212
Special Treatment	217
Toppings, Fillings, Glazes	221
BREAKFAST AND BRUNCH SANDWICHES	229
BREAKFAST BUFFETS	243
CHOLESTEROL AND THE BREAKFAST MENU	251
INDEX	253

ACKNOWLEDGEMENTS

THERE ARE MANY people to thank for the recipes that make up this book.

I am most grateful to the many capable technicians who worked in the various test kitchens to create and perfect these recipes. And to my valued business and professional associates with food processors, manufacturers, public relations firms, advertising agencies, associations and institutions who supplied recipe material for Volume Feeding Management Magazine during the years it was a separate publication. I also wish to express my thanks for their generous help in providing the photographs which illustrate this book.

Special thanks are also due to the foodservice operators who, time after time, graciously shared highly prized recipes from their kitchens.

And to Book Editor, Mrs. Jule Wilkinson, goes my sincere appreciation for her help in designing, editing and taking care of countless details relative to publishing this book.

Eulalia C. Blair

INTRODUCTION

THIS BOOK is planned with the thought of providing a helping hand to people concerned with foodservice at breakfast, brunch and coffee break time.

It carries a selection of over 240 recipes for breakfast and brunch items which range from fruits and juices to hearty meat and fish dishes. There are recipes for French toast, breakfast sandwiches and eggs; pancakes, waffles, fruit sauces and syrups, and a long, long list of delicious hot breads.

The wide range of recipes for doughnuts, coffee cakes, muffins, kuchens and Danish suggest items to promote for coffee breaks.

The book projects imaginative ways to escape a menu bound with tradition and put new spirit into the breakfast scheme. It includes ideas for inviting presentations, suggestions for buffets, special group breakfasts, and brunches planned around a regional theme. Withal, it directs attention to any number of pleasing touches that can make breakfast a more interesting—and successful—meal.

BREAKFAST AND BRUNCH DISHES

An Appealing Breakfast Presentation

Cling Peach Advisory Board

BREAKFAST

BREAKFAST POSES a different challenge than other meals. It comes at the time of day when most people are in a hurry, or still a little sleepy, or both. And—compared to other times—it's when they are inclined to be impatient, choosey, and set in their ways.

There may seem to be another problem (or is it an excuse?). Breakfast menus do not appear to allow too great a scope. As tradition dictates, there are relatively few items that find acceptance as breakfast fare. Within that limited frame, breakfast narrows down to become a highly personalized affair.

Individual breakfast eating habits tend to find and follow some definite groove. And people are likely to hold to pretty much the same pattern day after day. Moreover, the items that make up this particular breakfast must be "just so"—eggs perfectly timed, toast buttered or dry, blazing hot coffee—and served right away.

All in all, breakfast is a "different" meal. Nonetheless, it is an important one from both a nutritional and social point of view. There's plenty of rewarding potential, too, for operators who are willing to study patrons' whims, cater to their wishes, and do so with a genuine smile. There's no better time than now to move in and make it a more attractive meal.

At breakfast, as at any other time, it is up to you to provide your patrons with the particular "extra" they are looking for. This might be extra speed, extra service, extra variety, extra flavor, extra food value, extra economy. Or, it might be something else. Study it. Listen to your customers' comments. Observe the things they are asking for. The "extras" wanted in the morning may be different from those sought later in the day. Also, they can be quite different now than they were last year, or even a month ago!

Nearly everyone is time-conscious at breakfast. Most people are in a hurry. They want a breakfast that's quickly served and quickly eaten. But it's possible that this is not the major customer requisite. Everyone favors an eating place that radiates cheer; one that is orderly and faultlessly clean, with a menu card that's spotless. (To achieve this, the menu-imprinted placemat is a special boon.)

What's more, anyone, to enjoy the meal, has to feel welcome. The "Good Morning" greeting, agreeably spoken, can communicate, "We're glad you are here." When selecting your breakfast crew, weigh the qualities of friendliness, even temperament and a contagious smile. The breakfast shift is not for the employee who looks on the morning hours with loathing. An unhappy attitude, especially one of being "put-upon," comes across to customers at once, and is strongly resented. Don't run the risk of impairing your image this way!

A good cup of coffee can prove a marvelous force in extending a welcome if it is offered to customers as soon as they sit down. Coffee lovers also appreciate having their cups replenished throughout the meal. One way to insure having refills as soon as they are needed (and at the same time promote good will) is to put a full pot on each table and let customers help themselves as they like.

For success in today's fast changing world, it pays operators to keep abreast—or better yet, to anticipate—new breakfast trends. Make provision for the calorie-conscious crowd, and for those who search a menu with cholesterol content in mind. Give thought to people who have become devoted to meal-making breakfast drinks . . . to the fast-growing number of yoghurt fans.

Be prepared to serve iced coffee throughout the warm summer months. Have cola beverages and other soft drinks available since they rate high among menu choices.

There are any number of special touches that can make breakfast a more interesting—and more successful—meal. To list a few:

Provide a choice of tea, hot cocoa, postum and decaffeinated coffee as well as the best regular coffee. Have skim milk as well as whole milk available.

Offer a choice of cream, half and half, milk or skim milk for cereal.

Schedule a small garnish for egg dishes and fruit.

Provide a shaker of cinnamon and sugar for make-your-own cinnamon toast.

Offer brown sugar and a pat of butter with hot cereals.

Provide whipped butter with pancake and waffle orders.

Sprinkle a dusting of confectioners' sugar over French toast.

Offer a choice of jams, jellies, marmalade and comb honey.

Serve hash brown potatoes with egg orders.

Offer cream to accompany prunes, sliced fruits and berries.

Provide a small pipkin of melted butter, or a pitcher of syrup or honey blended with melted butter, for pancakes and waffles.

Warm the syrup (plain, flavored or fruited) as an added plus for pancakes and waffles.

Serve hot biscuits with comb or strained honey.

Give patrons a bonus with their breakfast order in the form of small Danish pastries offered from a tray.

Roll warm doughnuts and crullers in cinnamon sugar.

Serve warm baked apples and warm spiced applesauce.

6   BREAKFAST AND BRUNCH DISHES

Eye-Opening Breakfast Fruits

National Cherry Growers and Industries Foundation

Sunkist Growers, Inc.

FRUITS · JUICES · BEVERAGES

FRUIT JUICES AND FRUITS are generally considered the first step to a good breakfast. Fruit juices and fruit flavored breakfast drinks are both popular and convenient to serve. With the variety available, the choices you offer need never be run-of-the-mill. Besides the juices that can be squeezed from fresh fruit, there are many canned, frozen and bottled products on the market. Some of these combine two or more juices. You can also devise other interesting blends by simply mixing your own.

But be sure not to get so carried away with the advantages of juices and nectars as to neglect patrons who prefer to have their fruit as fruit, an item to eat rather than drink. There is a wide variety of fresh fruits on the market at most times of the year. Besides, there's always an attractive selection of canned and frozen fruits to round out your breakfast time offerings. Canned fruits, refrigerated in the can, are ready to serve in a flash.

With a little imagination, and a minimum of effort, there are many things that you can do to set your fruit service apart. You can, for example, offer a breakfast fruit cup; make a compote by grouping two or three fruits in a dish, side by side, unmixed; serve sliced fresh fruits in a companionable juice; fill pieces of melon with berries; serve warm baked apples with cream; broil grapefruit with syrup or spice; and give fruits a glamorous garnish to bolster appeal.

Check the following refresher lists to make sure you are taking advantage of the full potential of fruits that are popular with breakfast patrons.

JUICES
Apple juice (chilled; hot spiced)
Apple and cranberry juice
Apricot nectar
Breakfast drinks (fruit flavors)
Cocktail vegetable juice
Cranberry juice
Grape juice
Grapefruit juice
Orange juice
Pear nectar
Pineapple juice
Prune juice
Sauerkraut juice
Tangerine juice
Tomato juice (chilled; hot)
White grape juice (plain; with cassis)

FRUITS REQUIRING LITTLE OR NO PREPARATION

CANNED
  Applesauce
  Baked apples
  Kadota figs
  Fruit cocktail
  Grapefruit sections
  Mandarin orange sections (served plain or dished with prunes)
  Mixed fruits for salad
  Pineapple chunks
  Prunes
  Whole peeled apricots (plain or dished with prunes)

CHILLED OR FROZEN
  Grapefruit sections (fresh, chilled)
  Grapefruit and orange sections (fresh, chilled)
  Pineapple (frozen)

FRESH
  Whole ripe bananas
  Dark sweet cherries on stem
  Bunches of light or dark grapes
  Whole pears
  Whole tangerines

FRUITS REQUIRING A SMALL AMOUNT OF PREPARATION
Sliced bananas
Banana chunks in cranberry juice
Sliced bananas with whole strawberries
Sliced bananas with frozen pineapple
Banana chunks sauced with frozen strawberries
Blueberries
Blueberries and banana slices
Sliced bananas in orange juice

Fresh figs with cream
Grapefruit halves
Grapefruit sections sauced with frozen strawberries
Fruit kebabs (prunes, banana or pineapple chunks, whole strawberries)
Mandarin orange sections with banana slices
Pineapple chunks in orange juice
Melon halves or wedges
Orange halves
Plates of assorted small fresh fruits (apricots, plums, finger bananas, small bunches of grapes, cherries on stem, etc.)
Papaya halves
Strawberries
Uncapped whole strawberries with sugar for dipping

FRUITS REQUIRING A MODERATE AMOUNT OF PREPARATION

FRESH FRUITS
Fresh fruit cup
Sliced oranges
Orange sections with pineapple bits
Sliced peaches
Broiled grapefruit halves
Assorted melon balls
Honeydew wedge filled with cut fresh fruits
Cantaloupe halves filled with berries
Cantaloupe ring heaped with melon balls
Blueberries with sliced peaches
Fresh pineapple cubes served in shell
Fresh pineapple slices or fans
Raspberries with sliced peaches
Strawberries and cubed pineapple

COOKED FRUITS
Simmered dried apricots
Apricots and prunes, dished half and half
Prunes with lemon or lime
Prunes garnished with a thick half slice of orange (with rind)
Baked apples
Stewed apples with raisins
Mixed dried fruits
Hothouse rhubarb
Prunes and hothouse rhubarb, dished half and half
Hothouse rhubarb and banana slices, dished half and half
Poached whole peeled pear (with stem)
Cold fruit soup
Warm mixed fruit compote

HONEYDEW BOATS FILLED WITH CITRUS SECTIONS

Yield: 24 portions

Ingredients
HONEYDEW MELONS (6's)	4
GRAPEFRUIT (48's)	5
ORANGES (120's)	6
MINT	2 bunches

Procedure
   1. Cut each honeydew melon in half; remove seeds. Cut each half into 3 boat-shaped wedges.
   2. Section grapefruit and oranges.
   3. Arrange citrus segments in honeydew melon "boats" alternating 2 segments of grapefruit with 3 of orange.
   4. Garnish with a sprig of fresh mint.

SCALLOPED APPLES

Yield: 24 5-1/2 ounce portions

Ingredients
APPLE SLICES	1 No. 10 can
SUGAR, LIGHT BROWN	1 pound
BREAD CRUMBS, fine	2-1/4 cups
BUTTER or MARGARINE	1/2 pound
SALT	1/8 teaspoon

Procedure
   1. Place a shallow layer of apples and their juice in 2 well-buttered 9-inch by 15-inch pans to make a bottom layer of apples.
   2. Combine brown sugar and bread crumbs. Use half of crumb mixture to sprinkle over apples in the 2 pans. Dot with half the butter.
   3. Place remaining apples in pans, making a second layer of apples. Sprinkle with remaining crumbs. Dot with remaining butter. Add a sprinkle of salt to each pan.
   4. Bake in oven at 350°F. for 40 to 45 minutes or until the mixture starts to bubble. Run under broiler to brown.
   5. Serve hot with ham, sausages or bacon.

Spotlight Fruit at Breakfast

Sunkist Growers, Inc.

BROILED SHERRIED GRAPEFRUIT

Yield: 1 portion

Ingredients

GRAPEFRUIT HALF	1
SUGAR, BROWN	2 teaspoons
SHERRY	1 to 2 tablespoons
BUTTER	1 teaspoon
NUTMEG	dash

Procedure

    1. Cut around each section of fruit, loosening fruit from membrane. Do not cut around entire outer edge of fruit.

    2. Sprinkle with sugar. Pour sherry over top.

    3. Dot with butter. Sprinkle with nutmeg.

    4. Broil 3 inches from heat 15 to 20 minutes or until grapefruit is slightly brown and thoroughly heated through.

12 BREAKFAST AND BRUNCH DISHES

COLOR WHEEL PIZZA
(See picture, p. 2)

Yield: 6 12-inch pizza

Ingredients

SWEET DOUGH or	
RICH ROLL DOUGH	3-3/4 pounds
*BASIC PEACH FILLING	3 quarts
BASIC FRUIT COCKTAIL FILLING	3 quarts
BASIC SWEET ROLL ICING	as needed

Procedure

1. Scale dough into six 10-ounce pieces; round up. Let rest 10 minutes.

2. Roll out dough to fit bottoms and sides of greased 12-inch pizza pans. Pierce dough with fork.

3. Make a cross-separator with 2 pieces of cardboard about 11 inch by 1 inch. Slit each in center half way; fit together. Place in one pan over dough.

4. Ladle 1 cup (10 ounces) basic peach filling into each of two opposite quarters. Ladle 1 cup (10 ounces) basic fruit cocktail filling into each remaining quarter. Repeat for remaining 5 pans.

5. Bake in oven at 425°F. for 15 to 17 minutes, until crust is browned. Cool.

6. Drizzle icing on edge of each pizza.

*See recipes facing page.

Make Melon a Breakfast Special

Western Growers Assn.

*BASIC PEACH FILLING

Yield: approximately 3 quarts

Ingredients

CLING PEACH SLICES	1 No. 10 can
SUGAR	8 ounces
PREGELATINIZED STARCH (INSTANT)	2 ounces
LEMON POWDER	1/2 ounce
CORN SYRUP, LIGHT	6 ounces
ALMOND EXTRACT	1/2 teaspoon
BUTTER or MARGARINE, melted	4 ounces
EGG COLOR	as needed

Procedure

1. Drain peaches, reserving syrup.
2. Chop peaches coarsely.
3. Blend sugar, starch and lemon powder together. Beat into peach syrup.
4. Blend in corn syrup, almond extract and melted butter. Add peaches and egg color to give desired yellow color.

*BASIC FRUIT COCKTAIL FILLING

Yield: approximately 3 quarts

Ingredients

FRUIT COCKTAIL	1 No. 10 can
RED CINNAMON CANDIES	8 ounces
SUGAR	8 ounces
PREGELATINIZED STARCH (INSTANT)	2 ounces
LEMON POWDER	1/2 ounce
CORN SYRUP, LIGHT	6 ounces
RED FOOD COLORING (optional)	as needed

Procedure

1. Drain fruit cocktail, reserving syrup.
2. Add cinnamon candies to syrup. Heat and stir until dissolved. Cool.
3. Blend sugar, starch and lemon powder together. Beat into cinnamon syrup. Add corn syrup, fruit and, if desired, red coloring.

HOT BUTTERED APPLES

Yield: 30 portions (4 wedges each)

Ingredients

APPLES, COOKING (NORTHERN SPY) unpeeled, cored, cut into 6 wedges	1 gallon (20 apples)
SUGAR	2 cups
BUTTER	1/4 pound
RED FOOD COLORING	4 drops
WATER	1-1/2 cups

Procedure

    1. Spread apple wedges in a 12-inch by 18-inch pan.

    2. Combine sugar, butter, coloring and water in saucepan; bring to boil. Pour syrup over apples.

    3. Bake in oven at 350°F. until tender but not soft.

KOOSHAB (ARMENIAN FRUIT COMPOTE)

Yield: approximately 16 portions

Ingredients

RAISINS, SEEDLESS	1/2 pound
PEARS, DRIED	1/2 pound
APRICOTS, DRIED	1/2 pound
PRUNES, DRIED	1/2 pound
WATER, cold	as needed
CLOVES, WHOLE	1 tablespoon
MINT LEAVES	few
LEMON JUICE	1 tablespoon

Procedure

    1. Wash fruit thoroughly; drain.

    2. Put fruit in a saucepan; cover with cold water. Add cloves and mint leaves.

    3. Bring slowly to a boil. Reduce heat; simmer 45 minutes. Add lemon juice; stir.

    4. Cool; refrigerate until thoroughly chilled.

    5. Serve in individual chilled dessert dishes.

Fruits, Juices, Beverages   15

FRUIT COMPOTE

Yield: 24 portions (4 apricot halves and juice, 2 prunes)

Ingredients
PRUNES, DRIED	48
APRICOTS, DRIED	96 halves
SUGAR (optional)	to taste

Procedure

   1. Wash dried fruits. Place in a 2-quart saucepan with just enough water to cover.

   2. Place over low heat; simmer until fruit is tender. Add sugar, if desired.

SPICED HOT FRUIT COMPOTE

Yield: approximately 48 portions

Ingredients
CLING PEACH HALVES (medium)	1 No. 10 can
PEAR HALVES (medium)	1 No. 10 can
MANDARIN ORANGE SECTIONS	2 quarts
CHERRIES, DARK SWEET, pitted, drained	1 No. 10 can
LEMON SLICES, thin, from	1 lemon
CLOVES, WHOLE	2 teaspoons
CINNAMON STICKS, 3-in.	4

Procedure

   1. Drain peaches, pears and orange sections, reserving syrup.

   2. Put fruit in shallow pan. Add drained cherries and lemon slices.

   3. Measure 1-3/4 quarts of mixed fruit syrup drained from peaches, pears and oranges. Include a small amount of syrup from cherries, if desired. Add cloves and cinnamon; bring to a boil; cover; simmer 10 minutes.

   4. Pour syrup over fruit. Place over low heat or, bake in oven at 350°F. for 20 to 25 minutes or until fruit is heated through. Baste 2 or 3 times while heating. Serve warm.

HOT SPICED FRUITS

Yield: 25 portions (2 pineapple chunks and 1 piece each of other fruits)

Ingredients

PINEAPPLE CHUNKS	1 No. 2 can (1 pound, 4 ounces)
KUMQUATS, PRESERVED	1 jar (1 pound, 4 ounces)
VINEGAR	1/4 cup
SUGAR, BROWN (packed measure)	1/4 cup
CLOVES, WHOLE	1 teaspoon
CINNAMON STICKS, 3 in. long	2
APRICOT HALVES, drained	1 No. 2-1/2 can (1 pound, 14 ounces)
PURPLE PLUMS, drained	2 cans (1 pound each)

Procedure

1. Drain pineapple and kumquats. Combine syrup with vinegar, brown sugar and spices. Bring to a boil; reduce heat; simmer 10 minutes.
2. Add pineapple chunks, kumquats, drained apricots and purple plums. Heat.
3. Serve as an accompaniment to grilled ham or Canadian bacon.

THREE-ON-THE-ROCKS

Yield: approximately 3 quarts

Ingredients

KRAUT JUICE	2 No. 2 cans
BEEF BROTH	2 10-1/2-ounce cans
VEGETABLE JUICE COCKTAIL	2 No. 2 cans

Procedure

1. Combine ingredients; chill.
2. Serve over ice cubes.

Fruits, Juices, Beverages

MOCHA-FLAVORED HOT COCOA

Yield: 1 portion

Ingredients
HOT COCOA MIX	1 envelope
INSTANT COFFEE	1 envelope
HOT WATER or MILK	2/3 cup

Procedure
    1. Empty contents of individual envelopes in cup. Fill cup with liquid, stirring to mix thoroughly. Or blend ingredients in an electric blender. Serve piping hot.

BANANA-ORANGE SHAKE

Yield: 1 portion

Ingredients
BANANA, ripe	1
ORANGE JUICE, thoroughly chilled	1 cup

Procedure
    1. Peel banana; mash with fork.
    2. Combine with orange juice in blender or electric fountain mixer. Mix until smooth and creamy. Serve at once.

CHOCOLATE BANANA MILK SHAKE

Yield: 1 portion

Ingredients
MILK, well chilled	1 cup
CHOCOLATE SYRUP	1 to 2 tablespoons
BANANA, ripe	1

Procedure
    1. Put milk and chocolate syrup in blender or electric fountain mixer; blend.
    2. Peel banana; mash with fork. Add to milk mixture; mix until smooth and creamy. Serve at once.

Crisp Cereals in the Forefront

Kellogg Co.

CEREALS

CEREALS OCCUPY a prominent place on the breakfast menu and menu planners find that variety is the appropriate password to the world of cereal lovers. There's an almost bewildering array of the ready-to-eat type made of different grains in various shapes and styles. Still, new-comers continue to appear on the market with improved products developed year after year. There are cereals that come pre-sweetened. There are packages for individual service as well as larger sizes, both with innovations in wrapping and sealing to insure keeping the products deliciously crisp.

The ready-to-cook cereals have also been improved and the choices expanded. New granular and flaked products have joined the old familiar standbys. Among the strides forward is the remarkable reduction in time that is now required to cook these cereals.

As a breakfast dish, cereals, both cooked and dry, provide room for new ideas that can vary their service in an exciting number of attractive ways. Experiment with suggestions such as those on the following page:

FOR READY-TO-EAT CEREAL
  Offer a selection of fresh fruit toppings from a cart, Lazy Susan or tray
  Serve with soft ice cream topped with fruit in these combinations:
    Corn flakes, ice cream, sliced peaches
    Rice cereal, ice cream, strawberries
    Sugar-coated cereal, ice cream, bananas and blueberries
  Serve with prunes; serve chilled soft custard in place of milk
  Serve with two fresh fruits
    Sliced bananas and peaches
    Blueberries and sliced peaches
    Banana slices and strawberries
    Sliced peaches and raspberries
    Banana slices and blackberries
  Top with sliced peaches or bananas; sprinkle with plain or toasted coconut
  Serve two or three kinds of cereal, side by side in bowl
  Serve corn flakes topped with bran flakes (with or without raisins)

FOR COOKED CEREAL
  Top with broiled canned peach slices
  Cook with part milk; add light or dark raisins, cut-up dates, dried apricots or dried figs
  Scatter finely crushed peanut brittle over the top
  Top with flaked coconut rubbed with grated orange peel
  Add a little vanilla to oatmeal
  Top farina with stewed apricot halves; serve with almond flavored light cream
  Add light or dark raisins and mashed banana to cereal after removing from heat
  Sprinkle with brown or maple sugar; place a pat of butter in center
  Place hot cereal in individual casseroles; top with miniature marshmallows; run under broiler to brown
  Top with a small scoop of strawberry ice cream
  Top with cherry preserves, jelly or orange marmalade
  Serve hot thick cereal in individual casseroles, using an ice cream scoop to portion it. Sprinkle with light brown

Spicy Hot Cereal with Fruit

The Quaker Oats Company

sugar blended with butter. Run under broiler to melt sugar and glaze

Present with brown sugar, cinnamon sugar or a drizzle of honey, light molasses or syrup in addition to milk or cream

Top with crushed graham crackers, a sprinkling of ready-to-eat cereal or Cereal Crunch Topping

BROILED PEACH SLICES WITH CEREAL

Yield: 24 portions

Ingredients
PEACHES, CANNED CLING SLICES	1-1/2 quarts
SUGAR or CINNAMON SUGAR	as needed
CEREAL, hot cooked or	3-3/4 quarts
READY-TO-EAT CEREAL, cold	24 ounces

Procedure
1. Drain peaches; arrange in baking pan.
2. Sprinkle with sugar or cinnamon sugar. Broil until lightly browned.
3. Keep warm on steam table. Top 5-ounce portion hot cereal or 1-ounce portion of ready-to-eat cereal with 2 ounces broiled peach slices.

BAKED GRITS

Yield: 24 portions, 2 3-quart casseroles or 2 10-inch by 12-inch by 2-inch pans

Ingredients
HOMINY GRITS	2 cups
MILK	2-1/2 qua
SALT	2-1/2 teaspoons
BUTTER or MARGARINE	6 tablespoons
PARSLEY, chopped	1/2 cup
EGG YOLKS, beaten	6
PAPRIKA	1/2 teaspoon
EGG WHITES	6
SALT	1/4 teaspoon

Procedure
1. Cook first four ingredients over low heat until thick; cool slightly.
2. Add parsley, egg yolks and paprika; cool.
3. Beat egg whites with remaining salt until stiff. Fold into grits.
4. Turn into well-greased casseroles or pans.
5. Bake in a pan of hot water in oven at 350°F. for 1-1/4 hours.

SCALLOPED RICE

Yield: 12 portions

Ingredients
EGGS, beaten	6
MILK, SKIM	1 quart
NUTMEG	1/2 teaspoon
SALT	1 teaspoon
SUGAR	2 tablespoons
RICE, cooked	1 quart

Procedure
1. Combine eggs, milk, nutmeg, salt and sugar; mix well. Stir in rice.
2. Turn into a buttered 12-inch by 9-inch by 2-1/2-inch pan. Cover pan with foil. Set pan in hot water. Bake in oven at 350°F. for 35 minutes or until done.
3. Let stand about 10 minutes before serving.
4. Serve with ham or bacon; or, as a side dish.

CEREAL CRUNCH TOPPING

Yield: 3-1/4 pounds mixture

Ingredients
BUTTER	12 ounces
SUGAR, BROWN	1-1/2 pounds
FLOUR	2 ounces
WHOLE WHEAT FLAKES	1 pound (3-3/4 quarts)

Procedure
1. Melt butter in a heavy saucepan. Combine brown sugar and flour; add to butter. Cook and stir over low heat 2 minutes or until sugar melts but does not bubble.
2. Add flakes; mix quickly and thoroughly to coat all flakes. Spread thin in shallow pan. Cool.
3. Crumble coarsely and sprinkle over cooked cereal, applesauce, sliced fresh peaches or bananas. Or, crumble finely and sprinkle over quick coffee cakes or muffins, pressing topping well into batter.

RICE CROQUETTES WITH HOT SPICED APPLESAUCE

Yield: 50 portions

Ingredients

RICE	2-1/2 pounds
SALT	3 tablespoons
CAYENNE PEPPER	1/4 to 1/2 teaspoon
APPLE JUICE	3 quarts
CHEESE, CHEDDAR, diced	3 pounds
EGGS, beaten	2 pounds
CRACKER CRUMBS	2 cups
ONION JUICE	1/4 cup
WORCESTERSHIRE SAUCE	3 tablespoons
PARSLEY, chopped	3 cups
CEREAL FLAKES	6 quarts
APPLESAUCE	1-1/2 No. 10 cans
CINNAMON	4 teaspoons

Procedure

    1. Cook rice with salt and cayenne in apple juice until rice is tender and juice has been absorbed. Remove from heat.

    2. Combine rice with cheese, eggs, cracker crumbs, onion juice, Worcestershire and parsley.

    3. Cool thoroughly.

    4. Crush cereal flakes lightly.

    5. Shape rice mixture into 100 croquettes using No. 24 scoop.

    6. Roll in cereal; place on greased baking sheet.

    7. Bake in oven at 425°F. for 10 minutes.

    8. Combine applesauce and cinnamon. Heat. Serve hot over rice croquettes, allowing 2 ounces per portion.

Cereals 25

Figs with Unique Flavor as Starters

Glorietta Brand by Santa Clara Packing Company

Cereal and Fruit in Tempting Tandem

National Cherry Growers and Industries Foundation

Serve-Yourself Breakfast Meat

Armour and Company

Armour and Company

MEAT, CHICKEN AND FISH

BACON, HAM and Canadian bacon are favorite breakfast items alone or in partnership with pancakes, waffles, French toast, and any style of eggs. So are pork sausages and sausage cakes. Scrapple, corned beef hash, and creamed chipped beef are other welcome candidates for the breakfast list.

Operators catering to robust appetites may do well by featuring hamburger patties, broiled lamb chops or steaks of small dimensions as well as a choice of fish. Offerings such as apples and sausage en brochette, eggs scrambled with crisp bacon bits, chicken-filled crepes, and an omelet filled with creamed diced ham will please the more sophisticated taste.

A Hearty Breakfast Combination

Armour and Company

SAUSAGE NOODLE CASSEROLE

Yield: 54 portions

Ingredients

NOODLES, MEDIUM FINE	2 pounds
ONION, chopped	1/2 cup
BACON DRIPPINGS	1/2 cup
CARROTS, RAW, ground	8 medium
CREAM OF MUSHROOM SOUP	1 51-ounce can
MILK	2 cups
SALT	1 tablespoon
PEPPER	1/2 teaspoon
LINK SAUSAGE, fully cooked	6 pounds

Procedure

1. Cook noodles in boiling salted water until just tender, about 8 minutes. Drain.
2. Lightly brown the onion in bacon drippings.
3. Combine noodles, onion, ground carrots, mushroom soup, milk, salt and pepper. Pour into baking pan.
4. Arrange sausage links over the top. Bake in oven at 350°F. for 30 minutes until sausage is heated and the noodle mixture is hot. (This does not brown.)

COUNTRY SAUSAGE AND APPLE RINGS

Yield: 32 portions

Ingredients

FRESH PORK SAUSAGE	10 pounds
*BAKED APPLE RINGS	64

Procedure

1. Shape sausage into round patties 3/8-inch thick, 2-1/2 oz. each. Cook in skillet until well browned and thoroughly done.
2. Place one apple ring on each sausage patty. Serve immediately.

*BAKED APPLE RINGS

Ingredients

APPLES	12
MARGARINE	2 ounces
SUGAR	4 ounces
HOT WATER	2 cups
MARGARINE, melted	2 ounces
SUGAR	4 ounces
CINNAMON	1 teaspoon

Procedure

1. Core apples and slice into rings 3/8-inch thick.
2. Spread margarine on shallow pans.
3. Mix first amount of sugar and water, pour into pans.
4. Place apple rings flat in pans. Brush rings with melted margarine.
5. Mix remaining sugar and cinnamon, sprinkle over apples.
6. Bake just before serving. Bake in oven at 325°F. until tender, about 10 minutes.

OVEN-BAKED PANCAKES WITH SAUSAGE

Yield: 40 portions

Ingredients
FLOUR	1 pound, 12 ounces
BAKING POWDER	1/3 cup
SUGAR	6 tablespoons
SALT	4 teaspoons
EGGS	12
MILK	1-1/2 quarts
SHORTENING, melted	3/4 cup
LINK SAUSAGES, fully cooked	4 pounds

Procedure

1. Sift flour, baking powder, sugar and salt.
2. Beat eggs until light. Add milk and shortening; beat.
3. Add sifted dry ingredients slowly to the liquid. Beat until batter is smooth.
4. Pour into 4 greased 10-1/2-inch by 15-1/2-inch by 1-inch pans. Arrange sausage links on the batter. Bake in oven at 450°F. for 15 minutes or until done.
5. Cut each pan in 10 portions. Serve hot with butter and syrup or apricot sauce.*

*APRICOT SAUCE

Yield: approximately 3-1/8 quarts

Ingredients
SUGAR	1/2 cup
CORNSTARCH	1/4 cup
APRICOT NECTAR	3 quarts
LEMON JUICE	1/2 cup

Procedure

1. Combine sugar and cornstarch. Add nectar and lemon juice. Cook and stir about 5 minutes or until sauce is thickened and clear.

BAKED MEAT SANDWICH

Yield: 1 pan, 12-inch by 18-inch

Ingredients

FILLING

PORK, ground	4 pounds
ONION, chopped	2 cups
CHEESE, PARMESAN, grated	1 cup
CHEESE, SWISS, grated	2 cups
EGGS, beaten	4
LIQUID HOT PEPPER SEASONING	1 teaspoon
SALT	2 tablespoons
PARSLEY, chopped	6 tablespoons

CRUST

BISCUIT MIX	2-1/2 pounds
WATER	2-1/4 cups
MAYONNAISE	1 cup
EGG YOLK, beaten (to brush top)	as needed

Procedure

1. Cook pork and onion over low heat until pork is not pink. Do not brown.
2. Cool mixture; add cheeses, beaten eggs, hot pepper seasoning, salt and parsley; mix.
3. Place biscuit mix in bowl. Add water and mayonnaise. Blend 1 minute on low speed or mix by hand.
4. Pat 1/2 of dough evenly into bottom of a 12-inch by 18-inch pan. Spread with cooled meat filling.
5. Spread remaining dough over filling. Brush with beaten egg yolk.
6. Bake in oven at 400°F. for 20 to 25 minutes or until done.
7. Cut into squares. Serve hot.

SCRAPPLE

Yield: 16 to 18 loaves (8-inch by 4-inch by 3-inch)

Ingredients	
LIVER, PORK	3-1/2 pounds
PORK	4-1/2 pounds
BROTH AND WATER	3-1/4 gallons
SHORTENING	1 pound
CORN MEAL, YELLOW	2-1/4 pounds
SALT	6 ounces
PEPPER	1/2 ounce
FLOUR, PASTRY	9 ounces
FLOUR, BUCKWHEAT	2 pounds, 13 ounces

Procedure

1. Boil liver and pork until tender. Drain, reserving broth. Grind liver and pork (not too fine).

2. Add water to broth to make required amount. Add ground liver and pork and shortening.

3. Mix corn meal, salt and pepper. Add to meat mixture; bring to a boil. Add flour.

4. Cook slowly; add buckwheat flour, small amounts at a time, until the desired consistency. (It may not take all of the buckwheat flour.)

5. When thick, pour into loaf pans. Cool. Refrigerate overnight.

6. Cut in 1/4-inch slices. Fry in hot fat until brown and crusty on both sides.

CREAMED HAM AND MUSHROOMS

Yield: 25 1-cup portions

Ingredients

CREAM OF MUSHROOM SOUP (CANNED)	3 quarts
TOMATO SAUCE	3 cups
GREEN PEPPERS, cut in slivers	1-1/2 quarts
BUTTER or MARGARINE	6 ounces
HAM, cooked, diced	3 quarts
PATTY SHELLS	25
EGGS, hard-cooked, chopped	1-1/2 cups

Procedure

1. Combine soup and tomato sauce; heat.
2. Saute peppers in butter 3 to 5 minutes.
3. Add peppers and ham to soup mixture. Let stand 10 to 15 minutes to blend flavors, keeping hot for service.
4. Serve in patty shells; garnish with chopped egg.

HAM WITH CARROT-PINEAPPLE SAUCE

Yield: 50 portions

Ingredients

CANNED HAM, sliced	10 pounds (50 slices, 2 to 3 ounces each)
PINEAPPLE, crushed	1-3/4 quarts
CARROTS, shredded	3 cups
SUGAR, BROWN	6 ounces (1 cup, packed)
CINNAMON	1/2 teaspoon
CLOVES	1 teaspoon
CORNSTARCH	1/4 cup

Procedure

1. Arrange about 17 slices of ham in each of 3 9-inch by 12-inch by 2-inch baking pans.
2. Combine pineapple, carrots, brown sugar, cinnamon, cloves and cornstarch. Mix thoroughly. Cook until mixture boils and thickens.
3. Pour sauce over ham. Bake in oven at 350°F. for 30 minutes.

Ham and Egg Pie with Asparagus

Pillsbury Co.

ESCALLOPED HAM AND APPLES

Yield: 36 portions

Ingredients	
SUGAR, BROWN	1-1/2 pounds
CLOVES, GROUND	2 teaspoons
APPLES, sliced	1 No. 10 can
HAM, cut in 1/2-inch cubes	10 pounds
CORNSTARCH	2/3 cup
WATER	3 cups
LEMON JUICE	1 cup
BREAD CRUMBS, soft	1 quart
BUTTER, melted	1/3 cup

Procedure
1. Combine brown sugar and cloves.
2. Arrange apples, sugar mixture and ham in alternate layers in shallow baking pans.
3. Blend cornstarch and cold water. Heat and stir until mixture thickens and clears. Remove from heat; stir in lemon juice. Pour over top of pans.
4. Bake in oven at 325°F. for 45 minutes to 1 hour.
5. Toss crumbs with melted butter; sprinkle evenly over tops of pans. Continue baking for 20 minutes or until crumbs are brown.

HAM AND SWEETBREADS FLORENTINE

Yield: 48 portions

Ingredients	
CREAM SAUCE, medium, hot	2 gallons
MUSTARD, DRY	1-1/2 tablespoons
GREEN PEPPER	6 ounces
PIMIENTO, chopped	9 ounces
ONION, chopped (reconstituted instant)	4-1/2 ounces
SWEETBREADS, cooked, diced 1/2-inch	3 pounds, 12 ounces
HAM, cooked, diced 1/2-inch	3 pounds, 12 ounces
SPINACH	27 pounds
SALT	3 ounces
ONION, chopped (reconstituted instant)	12 ounces
GARLIC, minced	3 cloves
WATER, boiling	1 gallon
PAPRIKA	as needed

Procedure

1. Combine cream sauce, dry mustard, green pepper, pimiento and first amount of onion. Add sweetbreads and ham. Keep hot.

2. Cook spinach as needed. Chop spinach coarsely. Add spinach, salt, remaining onion and garlic to boiling water. Cook until tender but do not overcook. Drain thoroughly. Keep hot.

3. To serve, spread 6 ounces spinach on bottom and sides of hot casserole dish. Put 8 ounces creamed mixture in center, leaving a ring of spinach around sides. Sprinkle a little paprika on top. Serve immediately.

HAM BALLS IN SOUR CREAM GRAVY

Yield: 50 portions

Ingredients
COOKED HAM, ground	8 pounds (1-3/4 gallons)*
ONIONS, chopped	2 cups
PEPPER	2 teaspoons
EGGS	8

*A 16-pound fully cooked ham is sufficient.

Procedure

1. Combine all ingredients. Shape into 100 balls, approximately 1/4 cup per ball.
2. Place in 4 baking pans 9-inch by 12-inch by 2-inches; 25 balls per pan. Bake in oven at 400°F. for 35 to 40 minutes.
3. Serve with sour cream gravy. (See recipe below.)

SOUR CREAM GRAVY

Yield: 3 quarts

Ingredients
SHORTENING	1 cup
FLOUR	1 cup
WATER	1 quart
SOUR CREAM	2 quarts
DILL SEED	2 teaspoons
MARJORAM	2 teaspoons

Procedure

1. Melt shortening; add flour. Cook until bubbly.
2. Add water, sour cream, dill seed and marjoram. Cook and stir until mixture boils.
3. Reduce heat; continue cooking for 10 minutes. Serve on Ham Balls.

Hearty Brunch Trio

Pillsbury Food Service

PRUNE JAMBALAYA

Yield: 50 3/4-cup portions

Ingredients

ONION, chopped	3 cups
CELERY, diced	1-1/4 quarts
BACON FAT	2/3 cup
HAM, cooked, 1/2-inch cubes	5 pounds
RICE, uncooked	1 quart
PRUNES, pitted, chopped	2-1/2 quarts
HAM STOCK	3 quarts
CHILI SAUCE	1 cup
GREEN PEPPERS, chopped	1 cup
SALT	2 tablespoons
WORCESTERSHIRE SAUCE	1/2 cup

Procedure
1. Saute onion and celery in bacon fat until lightly browned.
2. Add remaining ingredients; heat to boiling. Cover; simmer, stirring frequently, until rice is tender and liquid is absorbed.

Eggs in Hash-Based Potato Nests

Smith, Bucklin and Associates

SPAGHETTI WITH CHICKEN LIVERS

Yield: 25 8-ounce portions

Ingredients

ONIONS, minced	1 cup
CHICKEN LIVERS, chopped	2 cups
BUTTER or MARGARINE	1/2 pound
FLOUR	1/4 cup
CHICKEN STOCK	1-1/2 quarts
TOMATO PASTE	2 cups
SALT	2 teaspoons
PEPPER	1/4 teaspoon
PIMIENTOS, minced	1/2 cup
SPAGHETTI, cooked	6 quarts
	(2 pounds uncooked)
CHEESE, grated	2 cups

Procedure
1. Saute onions and chopped livers in butter until lightly browned.
2. Add flour; blend until smooth.
3. Mix stock and tomato paste thoroughly; add to chicken liver mixture.
4. Add seasonings and pimientos; simmer 5 to 10 minutes.
5. Combine with spaghetti. Serve sprinkled with cheese.

ROAST BEEF HASH

Yield: 25 5-ounce portions

Ingredients

ROAST BEEF, 1/4-inch cubes	3 pounds
POTATOES, cooked (cold) cut in 3/8-inch dice	4 pounds
MARGARINE	2 ounces
ONIONS, 3/8-inch dice	2 cups
GREEN PEPPER, 3/8-inch dice	1 medium
TOMATOES, canned, broken up	2 cups
BROWN GRAVY	2 cups
SALT	1 teaspoon
BLACK PEPPER	1/2 teaspoon
BREAD CRUMBS	1/3 cup
PAPRIKA	as needed

Procedure

1. Use remnants and left-over pieces of roast beef. Trim off any hard crust and fat. Cut into 1/4-inch cubes.
2. Combine beef and potatoes.
3. Melt margarine; add onions and green peppers. Saute until golden brown.
4. Add tomatoes, brown gravy, salt and pepper. Bring to boil; add to beef and potato mixture; fold together.
5. Turn into 12-inch by 18-inch pan. Sprinkle with bread crumbs, then lightly with paprika.
6. Bake in oven at 400°F. for one hour.

PINEAPPLE HASH PIE ⟶

Yield: 4 9-inch pies

Ingredients
CORNED BEEF HASH	1 No. 10 can
CRUSHED PINEAPPLE, drained	1 quart
EGGS	6
MILK	3/4 cup
PARSLEY, chopped	1 cup
MUSTARD, PREPARED	1/4 cup
CLOVES, GROUND	1/2 teaspoon
PIE SHELLS, 9-inch, unbaked	4

CREAMED CHIPPED BEEF AND EGGS EN CASSEROLE

Yield: 25 portions

Ingredients
CHIPPED BEEF	2 pounds
CREAM	2 cups
CREAM SAUCE	3 quarts
BUTTER	1/4 pound
EGGS, hard-cooked, quartered	12
SALT	1 tablespoon
PEPPER	1 teaspoon
WORCESTERSHIRE SAUCE	2 tablespoons
PARSLEY, chopped	1/2 cup

Procedure

1. Boil chipped beef 2 to 3 minutes. Drain; combine with cream and cream sauce. Simmer 5 minutes or until sauce is of desired consistency.
2. Blend in butter. Add eggs.
3. Remove from heat; add seasonings and parsley.
4. Serve in casserole with toast points.

Procedure
1. Combine hash, pineapple, eggs, milk, parsley, mustard and cloves; mix well.
2. Turn 1 quart mixture into each unbaked pie shell.
3. Bake in oven at 350°F. for 40 to 45 minutes.
4. Let stand 15 minutes before cutting into wedges. Serve warm, reheating, if necessary.

Variation

Sprinkle grated cheddar cheese over top of pies during last 10 minutes of baking.

CORNED BEEF HASH WITH PEACHES

Yield: 27 portions

Ingredients

CORNED BEEF HASH	2 No. 10 cans
CLING PEACH HALVES, drained	27
SWEET PICKLE RELISH	1-1/2 cups
PREPARED MUSTARD	6 tablespoons

Procedure
1. Portion corned beef hash into individual baking dishes, allowing 8 ounces (1 cup) per portion. Make a slight indentation in center. Place peach half, cut side up, in center of hash.
2. Combine pickle relish and mustard. Spoon about 1 tablespoon mixture into each peach half.
3. Place baking dishes on sheet pans. Bake in oven at 350°F. for 20 minutes.

Variations

For **Sugar 'n Cream-Glazed Peaches and Hash,** omit pickle relish mixture. Blend 1/3 cup peach syrup, 2/3 cup light cream, 1/3 cup prepared mustard and 1/3 cup brown sugar. Spoon over peaches; bake as above.

For **Tangy Mustard-Glazed Peaches and Hash,** omit pickle relish mixture. Blend 2/3 cup brown sugar, 2 tablespoons dry mustard, 1/3 cup lemon juice and 1/2 teaspoon salt. Spoon over peaches, bake as above.

CREAMED CHICKEN JOSEPHINE

Yield: 5 gallons

Ingredients

CHICKEN FAT	14 ounces
FLOUR	14 ounces
CHICKEN BASE	1 cup
CHICKEN STOCK	1-1/2 gallons
MILK, EVAPORATED	1 gallon
CORNSTARCH	1 cup
WATER	as needed
SALT	as needed
PEPPER	as needed
GARLIC, GRANULATED	1 teaspoon
WORCESTERSHIRE SAUCE	1 tablespoon
MACE	1 teaspoon
EGG COLORING	as needed
CHICKEN, cooked meat from	12 5-pound hens
MUSHROOMS, CANNED	1 quart

Procedure

1. Blend chicken fat and flour. Add chicken base; mix thoroughly. Add chicken stock and evaporated milk. Cook and stir until sauce is thickened and smooth.

2. Blend cornstarch with enough water to make a thin, smooth paste. Add to hot sauce; continue to cook and stir until thickening is completed and starch is cooked.

3. Add seasonings. Add egg coloring to tint a delicate shade.

4. Add chicken and mushrooms. Heat.

5. Serve over patty shells.

CHICKEN-FILLED CREPES

Yield: 30 portions (2 crepes)

Ingredients

ONION, chopped	1 small
CELERY, diced	1 cup
BUTTER or MARGARINE	2 tablespoons
MUSHROOMS, diced	1 cup
BUTTER or MARGARINE, melted	8 ounces
FLOUR	1 cup
SALT	1-1/2 teaspoons
CREAM, 12%	3 cups
CHICKEN BROTH	3 cups
WINE, DRY, WHITE	1-1/2 cups
CHEESE, SHARP CHEDDAR, grated	3 cups (12 ounces)
PARSLEY, FRESH, minced	1/3 cup
CHICKEN, boned, finely chopped	1 36-ounce can
CREPES, baked (6-inch)	60

Procedure

1. Saute chopped onion and celery in first amount of butter until tender but not browned. Set aside.
2. Brown mushrooms in part of the melted butter. Remove mushrooms from pan.
3. Add remaining butter to pan; blend in flour and salt. Add cream and chicken broth. Cook and stir until thickened and smooth.
4. Add wine and half the cheese; stir until cheese melts. Combine reserved onion mixture and parsley with chicken.
5. Add about 1/4 cup of the sauce to chicken mixture or enough to moisten to spreading consistency.
6. Add mushrooms to remaining sauce.
7. Roll pancakes with filling. Place two filled crepes in each individual ovenware serving dish. Top with sauce, allowing 1/4 to 1/3 cup per portion.
8. Sprinkle with remaining cheese; place under broiler to thoroughly heat and brown.

BROILED LIVER

Yield: 24 portions

Ingredients

CALVES or BABY BEEF LIVER, 1/2-inch thick slices, 4 ounces each	24 slices
BACON SLICES, 1 ounce each	24 slices

Procedure

1. For each order: Place 1 slice of liver on a shallow pie pan. Place 1 strip of bacon over each slice of liver.
2. Broil 3 minutes at medium broiler heat. Turn liver; place bacon on top of liver again.
3. Broil 3 more minutes. Serve immediately.

CHICKEN LIVER SAUTE

Yield: 16 portions

Ingredients

ONION, chopped coarsely	4 ounces
MARGARINE	6 ounces
CHICKEN LIVER, trimmed	4 pounds
MUSHROOMS, sliced	12 ounces
SALT	2 teaspoons
PEPPER	1/4 teaspoon
CHICKEN STOCK	1-1/2 cups
SHERRY	1/4 cup
FLOUR	1 ounce
COLD WATER	1/3 cup

Procedure

1. Saute onions lightly in margarine. Add liver and mushrooms; sprinkle with seasonings. Cook until liver is almost done, about 5 minutes. Stir carefully to keep liver whole.
2. Add stock and wine, cook until liver is thoroughly done, about 3 minutes.
3. Drain stock from liver. Add flour mixed with water. Cook until thick and smooth. Pour over liver. Serve immediately on buttered toast.

LIVER ON RICE

Yield: 50 1/2-cup portions liver

Ingredients

DEHYDRATED CHOPPED ONIONS*	1/2 cup
WATER	3/4 cup
LIVER, cut julienne	4 pounds
FLOUR	1 cup
SALT	2 teaspoons
SHORTENING	3/4 cup
CELERY, chopped	1 quart
CREAM OF MUSHROOM SOUP, CONDENSED	2 51-ounce cans
MILK	3 cups
WORCESTERSHIRE SAUCE	3 tablespoons
PEPPER	1/2 teaspoon
RIPE OLIVES, chopped	2 cups
PIMIENTOS, cut in strips	1 cup
RICE, cooked	2 gallons

Procedure

   1. Cover onions with water; allow to stand 20 minutes. Drain, reserving liquid.

   2. Dredge liver in mixture of flour and salt. Brown in 1/2 cup of the shortening.

   3. Saute onions and celery in remaining shortening until tender.

   4. Blend onion liquid, soup, milk, Worcestershire and pepper. Heat. Add liver, sauteed vegetables, olives and pimientos. Reheat.

   5. Serve over hot, cooked rice.

*2 cups chopped fresh onions may be used in place of dehydrated onion and water.

CODFISH BALLS

Yield: 50 portions (2 2-ounce balls)

Ingredients

SALT CODFISH, BONELESS	5 pounds
WATER, boiling	2-1/2 quarts
INSTANT MASHED POTATOES	2 pounds (1 quart)
MILK, hot	3 cups
EGGS, unbeaten	1 pound (2 cups)
PEPPER	1/2 teaspoon
ONION, finely chopped	3/4 cup
PARSLEY, finely chopped	1/2 cup
LEMON JUICE	1/2 cup

Procedure

1. Freshen and cook codfish according to package directions. Cool; flake. (Amount of flaked fish should be about 4 pounds or 1 gallon.)

2. Pour boiling water into mixer bowl. Gradually add potatoes, whipping at medium speed until well blended (about 1 minute).

3. Add milk gradually, then eggs, whipping until light and fluffy. Mix in pepper, onions, parsley, lemon juice and codfish. Season with salt, if desired.

4. Shape into balls, using No. 20 scoop. If desired, roll in flour or other coating mixtures. Fry in deep fat at $375^{\circ}F$. about 3 minutes or until golden brown. Or, if desired, shape mixture into patties; brown on both sides on greased grill or in skillet.

5. Serve hot with tomato or egg sauce.

CRAB FISH CAKES

Yield: approximately 400 4-ounce cakes

Ingredients

MARGARINE	3 pounds, 8 ounces
FLOUR	4 pounds, 12 ounces
ONIONS, DEHYDRATED	8 ounces
GREEN PEPPER, DEHYDRATED	6 ounces
SALT	5-1/2 ounces
SEAFOOD SEASONING	3-1/4 ounces
MILK	26 pounds
FISH FILLETS	90 pounds
CRABMEAT	10 pounds
EGGS	36
BREAD CRUMBS, soft	7 pounds
PREPARED BREADING MIX	as needed

Procedure

1. Melt margarine; blend in flour, onions, green peppers, salt and seafood seasoning. Add milk; cook and stir until thick and smooth. Refrigerate until *thoroughly chilled.*

2. Bake fish fillets until lightly cooked. Cool; flake. Combine with crabmeat.

3. Put chilled white sauce mixture in mixer; add eggs and bread crumbs; blend. Add fish mixture; mix only until combined.

4. Turn into pans; chill at least 4 hours.

5. Shape into 4-ounce cakes; coat with breading mix. Refrigerate or freeze.

6. Fry in deep fat at 350°F.

BAKED FISH PATTIES

Yield: 48 portions

Ingredients

POTATOES, cooked, hot	8 pounds
BUTTER or MARGARINE	1/2 pound
PARSLEY FLAKES	1/2 cup
SALT	3 tablespoons
WHITE PEPPER	2 teaspoons
NUTMEG	1 teaspoon
EGGS	8
FISH, cooked, flaked	10 pounds

Procedure

1. Mash potatoes. Add butter, parsley flakes, salt, pepper and nutmeg.

2. Add eggs, one at a time, beating well after each addition. Add flaked fish.

3. Refrigerate mixture until cool.

4. Shape on floured board into 3-ounce patties. Place on greased baking sheet.

5. Bake in oven at 375°F. for 30 minutes or until lightly browned.

6. Serve 2 patties per portion with herbed egg sauce.*

*See recipe facing page.

*HERBED EGG SAUCE

Yield: 48 portions

Ingredients

MUSTARD, POWDERED	2 tablespoons
WATER, warm	2 tablespoons
CREAM SAUCE, rich	2-1/2 quarts
PARSLEY FLAKES	1/4 cup
DEHYDRATED CHIVES	1/4 cup
INSTANT ONION POWDER	1 tablespoon
EGGS, hard-cooked, diced	12

Procedure

1. Mix mustard with warm water; let stand 10 minutes for flavor to develop.

2. Heat cream sauce, stirring constantly. Add mustard and remaining ingredients.

POTATO SALMON PATTIES

Yield: 20 3-ounce patties

Ingredients

MASHED POTATOES, hot	1 quart
SALMON	1 quart (2 pounds)
CHEDDAR CHEESE, SHARP, grated	3/4 cup
CELERY, chopped	1/2 cup
GREEN PEPPER, chopped	1/2 cup
ONION, minced	1 teaspoon
SALT	1 teaspoon

Procedure

1. Mix ingredients together. Shape into patties allowing 3 ounces per patty. Chill thoroughly.

2. Fry on lightly greased griddle at high heat until golden brown, about 5 minutes per side.

Juice as a Good Beginning

Sunkist Growers, Inc.

SEASONED FRESH TROUT

Yield: 2 portions

Ingredients

TROUT, LARGE	2
MILK	as needed
SEASONED SALT	2 teaspoons
BASIL LEAVES	1/4 teaspoon
BLACK PEPPER, GROUND	dash
CORN MEAL, WHITE	as needed
BACON SLICES	4
BUTTER or MARGARINE	1 ounce
LEMON WEDGES	4

Procedure

1. Dip trout in milk.
2. Combine seasonings; sprinkle inside and outside of trout. Dip in corn meal.
3. Fry bacon until crisp. Drain; keep warm.
4. Add butter to bacon fat. Pan fry trout until done, turning once.
5. Serve garnished with bacon and lemon.

COCONUT-LEMON TROUT

Yield: 4 portions

Ingredients

COCONUT, GRATED, PACKAGED	1/2 cup
FLOUR	1/4 cup
SALT	1 teaspoon
LEMON RIND, grated	1 teaspoon
PEPPER	1/8 teaspoon
TROUT, LARGE	4
EGG, slightly beaten	1
SHORTENING	as needed
LEMON WEDGES	4

Procedure

1. Combine coconut, flour, salt, lemon rind and pepper.
2. Dip fish in egg; roll in coconut mixture.
3. Pan fry in shortening until done, turning once.
4. Serve garnished with lemon wedges.

OYSTER MUSHROOM BROCHETTE

Yield: 1 portion

Ingredients

MUSHROOM CAPS, LARGE	4
BACON, cut in squares	3 strips
OYSTERS, STANDARD	10
PAPRIKA	as needed
SALT	as needed
BUTTER	as needed
RICE, hot, cooked	3/4 cup

Procedure

1. Thread mushrooms, bacon squares and oysters on skewer. Sprinkle with salt and paprika to season.
2. Broil slowly, basting with butter until done.
3. Serve on a bed of rice. Garnish with peas and tomato wedges, if desired.

52   BREAKFAST AND BRUNCH DISHES

Pancakes, Thick or Thin

American Dairy Assn.

Pillsbury Co.

PANCAKES

PANCAKES ATTRACT customers with their perennial charm —and little wonder, when you stop to think of the tremendous capacity for variation and fascinating change-abouts that pancakes offer.

Broadly speaking, pancakes are classified as thin pancakes (crepes), baked in a pan or as thick pancakes (wheat cakes, flapjacks or griddle cakes), baked on a griddle.

The thin, delicate crepes permit rolling and folding without danger of cracking. They also allow making and baking far in advance. Combined with savory fillings, they offer possibilities for exciting entrees for brunch. Teamed with fruit fillings and sauces, they initiate an interesting line of offerings for the breakfast menu as well as for brunch.

Pancakes of the thick type, right off the griddle, are usually presented as a stack with butter and a syrup or other sweet sauce. But—and what's often overlooked—they can team with savory accessories with similar aplomb. Or take on all manner of variations by way of ingredient changes and additions to the batter. Some recipes vary the kind of flour, calling for wheat flour in combination with buckwheat, graham, whole wheat or corn meal. Rolled oats, bran cereals, cooked rice and bread crumbs also find their way into pancake batters.

Thick pancakes with additions of blueberries or chopped apple are perennial favorites. Sweet corn is another addition that most people like. Other possibilities include drained crushed pineapple, thinly sliced or mashed banana, diced dates or finely cut prunes. Thick pancakes can also be varied with chopped nuts, coconut and chocolate chips. For pancakes of a savory nature, cottage cheese, grated cheddar, minced ham, thin frankfurter slices and chopped ripe olives go over well.

New presentation twists can also heighten the drama. Some suggestions—

For crepes, use these fillings:

> Creamed chicken; dress with a cream sauce seasoned with curry powder; scatter flaked coconut over the top
>
> Creamed spinach; top with a sharp cheddar cheese sauce with flecks of diced pimiento
>
> Creamed mushrooms and chopped hard-cooked eggs; top with a sauce flavored with cheese; garnish with a flourish of crisp bacon bits
>
> An apricot, peach or cherry filling; top with a sauce made with the matching fruit

For regular pancakes:

> Cream butter and brown sugar to serve as a spread
>
> Offer a warm fruit sauce in lieu of syrup
>
> Stack, spreading jelly or one of the fruit pie fillings in between; finish the top with a dusting of confectioners' sugar or a spoonful of sweetened sour cream
>
> Team with a special sauce, in combinations like these:
> Cottage cheese pancakes with strawberry sauce
> Whole wheat pancakes with sherried fig sauce
> Chocolate chip pancakes with whipped cream and chocolate sauce
> Apple pancakes with hot spiced honey
> Gingerbread pancakes with fruited whipped cream
> Kernel corn pancakes with creamed chipped beef or ham
> Ripe olive pancakes with melted cheese sauce

Buttermilk pancakes with curried tuna between and on top

SUGAR 'N SPICE PANCAKES

Yield: 14 to 16 pancakes

Ingredients
PANCAKE BATTER	1 quart
CINNAMON	2 teaspoons
ALLSPICE	1 teaspoon
NUTMEG	1 teaspoon

Procedure
1. Combine pancake batter and spices; blend.
2. Bake as pancakes. Serve with Brown Sugar Whip.*

*BROWN SUGAR WHIP

Yield: 1-3/4 pounds

Ingredients
BUTTER or MARGARINE	1 pound
SUGAR, BROWN	12 ounces (2 cups, packed measure)
LEMON RIND, grated	1 tablespoon

Procedure
1. Cream butter until light and fluffy.
2. Gradually add brown sugar, continuing to beat.
3. Blend in lemon rind.

BLUEBERRY GRIDDLE CAKES

Yield: 5 quarts batter

Ingredients

FLOUR, ALL-PURPOSE	4 pounds
BAKING POWDER	3 ounces (1/2 cup)
SALT	1 tablespoon
SUGAR	1 cup
SHORTENING	10-1/2 ounces
MILK	3 quarts
EGGS, slightly beaten	8 (1-2/3 cups)
BLUEBERRIES, FRESH or FROZEN (unthawed)	1 quart

Procedure

1. Sift flour, baking powder, salt and sugar together.
2. Cut in shortening until mixture resembles coarse meal.
3. Add milk and eggs; stir only until smooth. Add blueberries, stirring only to distribute fruit.
4. Bake on hot griddle. Serve hot with butter and syrup or with blueberry sauce or cinnamon hard sauce.*

*CINNAMON HARD SAUCE

Yield: 1 quart

Ingredients

BUTTER, soft	1-1/2 pounds
CINNAMON, GROUND	2 teaspoons
VANILLA EXTRACT	2 teaspoons
SUGAR, CONFECTIONERS', sifted	1 pound, 2 ounces (1 quart)

Procedure

1. Cream butter with cinnamon.
2. Gradually blend in vanilla. Add sugar gradually, beating after each addition until well blended.
3. Serve at room temperature with blueberry griddle cakes.

BREAD CRUMB GRIDDLE CAKES

Yield: 25 portions

Ingredients

MILK, warm	3 quarts
BREAD CRUMBS, soft	2 quarts
SUGAR	2 tablespoons
CREAM	2 cups
EGG YOLKS, beaten	12 (1 cup)
FLOUR, ALL-PURPOSE, sifted	1 pound (1 quart)
BAKING POWDER	6 tablespoons
SALT	4 teaspoons
EGG WHITES	12 (1-1/2 cups)

Procedure

   1. Mix milk and bread crumbs. Cool.

   2. Add sugar, cream and well beaten egg yolks.

   3. Sift flour, baking powder and salt together. Add to bread crumbs mixture.

   4. Beat egg whites until stiff; fold into batter.

   5. Bake on a hot, well-greased griddle to a delicate golden brown on both sides.

   6. Serve with a hot fruit sauce, a cheese sauce, or soft maple sugar or syrup.

PANCAKE RECIPE WITH VARIATIONS

Yield: approximately 24 4-1/2-inch pancakes

Ingredients

For each variation, use 5 cups pancake batter or amount of batter from 1 pound dry pancake mix prepared according to package directions.

Apple Pancakes: Add 1 cup finely chopped cooking apples.

Banana Pancakes: Add 1/3 cup finely chopped or mashed ripe bananas.

Blueberry Pancakes: Add 1 cup fresh or frozen blueberries.

Coconut Pancakes: Add 1/4 cup moist maracoon coconut.

Crunchy Pancakes: Add 1/4 cup wheat flake cereal.

BUTTERMILK HOT CAKES ⟶

Yield: 8-1/2 gallons batter, 180 portions of 3 2-ounce cakes each

Ingredients

FLOUR, PASTRY	21 pounds
SUGAR	1-1/2 pounds
BAKING POWDER	10 ounces
SALT	6 ounces
SODA	6 ounces
BUTTERMILK* (facing page)	5 gallons
EGGS, beaten	3 quarts (72)
OIL, COOKING	2 quarts

OLIVE FLAPJACKS WITH CHEESE SAUCE

Yield: 24 portions

Ingredients

RIPE OLIVES, pitted, drained	1-1/2 quarts
CHEESE, PROCESS AMERICAN	3 pounds
SOUR CREAM	1-1/2 quarts
BUTTERMILK PANCAKE MIX	3-1/2 pounds
SEASONED SALT	1 tablespoon
EGGS	6
MILK	2-1/2 quarts
SALAD OIL	1-1/2 cups
GREEN PEPPER, diced	2 cups
ONION, finely chopped	3/4 cup

Procedure

    1. Chop olives coarsely; set aside.

    2. Cut cheese into pieces. Place in saucepan; mix in sour cream. Heat gently, stirring until cheese is melted and mixture is smooth.

    3. Combine pancake mix, seasoned salt, eggs and milk. Stir in oil until blended. Add olives, green pepper and onion.

    4. Bake pancakes allowing 1/4 cup batter for each.

    5. Serve pancakes hot with cheese sauce allowing 4 pancakes and about 1/2 cup sauce per portion.

Procedure

1. Sift flour, sugar, baking powder and salt together.
2. Dissolve soda in a portion of the buttermilk. Combine with remainder of buttermilk and eggs.
3. Add liquid mixture to sifted dry ingredients; mix just until flour is dampened. Add oil; mix to blend into batter.
4. Bake on a hot griddle, turning once.

*If using less than a full can of buttermilk, stir contents of can to mix thoroughly before measuring.

GINGERBREAD PANCAKES WITH FRUITED WHIPPED CREAM

Yield: 9 portions

Ingredients

GINGERBREAD MIX (INSTITUTIONAL TYPE)	12 ounces
PANCAKE MIX	4 ounces
WATER	14 ounces
EGGS	2
CREAM, heavy (for whipping)	2 cups
CONFECTIONERS' SUGAR	1/2 cup
FRUIT COCKTAIL, CANNED, drained	1-1/2 cups

Procedure

1. Scale gingerbread mix, pancake mix and water in bowl. Add eggs; blend until smooth.
2. Allowing 1/4 cup batter for each pancake, bake on pre-heated 375°F. griddle for about 1-1/2 minutes on each side.
3. Whip cream; fold in sugar.
4. For each portion: stack 2 pancakes with whipped cream and fruit cocktail between and on top.

Variations

Substitute sliced ripe bananas or well-drained canned sliced peaches for drained fruit cocktail.

CREPES

Yield: 160

Ingredients
FLOUR	1-1/2 pounds
SUGAR, CONFECTIONERS'	1/2 cup
SALT	1 tablespoon
EGGS	24
MILK	3 quarts
CREAM, LIGHT	2 cups
BUTTER, clarified	1 cup

APPLE PANCAKE STACKS

Yield: 50 portions, 3 6-inch pancakes, 3/4 cup sauce

Ingredients
APPLESAUCE	2 No. 10 cans
SAUSAGE MEAT, BULK, cooked, crumbled	3 quarts
SAUSAGE FAT	1-1/4 cups
FROZEN CONCENTRATED ORANGE JUICE, thawed	3 cups
PANCAKE MIX	4-3/4 pounds
FROZEN CONCENTRATED ORANGE JUICE, thawed	1-1/4 quarts
CREAM, LIGHT or EVAPORATED MILK	1 gallon + 3 cups
EGGS, well beaten	1 quart

Procedure

1. Mix applesauce, cooked sausage, sausage fat and first amount of orange juice. Heat until mixture bubbles.
2. Blend pancake mix with remaining orange juice, cream and eggs.
3. Bake pancakes using 1/4 cup batter for each cake.
4. For each portion, stack 3 pancakes with 1/4 cup applesauce mixture between and on top. Serve with maple syrup, if desired.

Procedure

1. Sift flour, sugar and salt together.
2. Combine eggs, milk and cream.
3. Stir dry ingredients into the liquid; mix well. Add butter. Let stand 30 minutes; strain. (The batter should have consistency of light cream.)
4. Pre-heat a 4-in. crepe pan; lightly brush with butter. Add 2 tablespoons batter. Swirl and tilt pan so bottom gets an even coat of batter.
5. Pour off any excess of batter. Cook on medium heat until underside is brown. Turn; brown lightly on other side.
6. Remove from pan; cover with wax paper or dry towel until ready to use.

RICE PANCAKES

Yield: 20 portions, 40 pancakes

Ingredients

FLOUR, ALL-PURPOSE	4 cups (1 pound)
BAKING POWDER	3 tablespoons
SALT	2 teaspoons
EGGS, beaten	4
MILK	3 cups
BUTTER, melted	4 ounces
HONEY	1/4 cup
RICE, cooked	1-1/2 quarts
STRAWBERRIES, sliced, sweetened	1-3/4 quarts

Procedure

1. Sift flour, baking powder and salt together.
2. Combine eggs, milk, butter and honey. Add to flour mixture all at once; stir only until flour is moistened (batter should be lumpy). Stir in rice.
3. Bake on hot griddle using scant 1/4 cup batter per pancake.
4. Serve hot with sweetened sliced strawberries.

DELICATE THIN PANCAKES

Yield: 2 quarts

Ingredients

EGGS	8
SALT	4 teaspoons
SUGAR	4 tablespoons
BREAD FLOUR, sifted	3 cups
COLD WATER	1 quart
20% CREAM	2 cups

Procedure

1. Using a high speed mixer, beat eggs very light. Add salt and sugar and beat lightly.
2. Measure flour and sift.
3. Add the water first, then the cream alternately with the flour, beating constantly.
4. Let stand for at least 30 minutes, beat again before making cakes.*
5. To bake: bake on well-buttered griddle. Contrary to the regular rule for turning pancakes, turn these cakes twice in order to have the smoother surface on the outside.
6. To serve: put a small amount of soft maple butter in the center of each cake and roll. Place 4 rolls side by side on a plate with 3 crisp bacon strips on top.

*Note

Beat the batter on the machine or by hand before each order. The longer the batter stands, and the more times it is beaten, the more tender the cakes.

HAM AND JAM PANCAKES

Yield: 25 5-ounce portions

Ingredients

BREAD CRUMBS, soft	2 quarts
HAM, cooked, finely chopped	1 quart
BUTTER or MARGARINE, melted	1/2 cup
MILK, scalded	1 quart
EGGS, beaten	8
SALT	2 teaspoons
PEPPER	1 teaspoon
JAM	1 quart

Procedure

1. Combine all ingredients except jam.
2. Bake on a hot greased griddle, dropping the cakes with a large spoon. Turn to brown both sides.
3. Spread jam on half of each cake; fold over and serve at once.

Note

These cakes are very delicate and require careful handling.

Pancake Sausage Rolls with Pineapple

The Quaker Oats Company

A Waffly Good Breakfast

Kellogg Co.

WAFFLES

THERE'S ANOTHER WORLD of variety in waffles: prepared from scratch, made from a mix or simply heated from the frozen state. A natural at breakfast, they can also star at brunch where they can provide a crisp basis for a savory creamed dish or fashion a dessert.

Here are a few of many ideas:

FOR BREAKFAST (OR BRUNCH)
  Plain waffles with a selection of syrups; accompany with
    bacon, sausage patties or ham
  Bacon waffles with honey butter
  Cinnamon waffles with blueberry sauce
  Pecan waffles with sliced peaches and maple syrup
  Peanut butter waffles with honey butter

AS AN ENTREE AT BRUNCH
  Sour cream waffles with creamed chipped beef and sliced
    mushrooms
  Kernel corn waffles with creamed chicken
  Curry waffles with creamed chicken or turkey
  Plain waffles with sherried shrimp
  Cheese waffles with creamed ham or vegetables a la king

66   BREAKFAST AND BRUNCH DISHES

AS A BRUNCH-TIME DESSERT
  Chocolate-nut waffles with ice cream and chocolate sauce
  Coconut waffles with butterscotch sauce
  Banana-nut waffles with sliced bananas and maple syrup
  Blueberry waffles with sour cream and warm blueberry sauce
  Plain waffles with whipped cream cheese and warm lemon sauce

Waffles with Maraschino Cherry Sauce

National Cherry Growers and Industries Foundation

WAFFLE RECIPE WITH VARIATIONS

Yield: approximately 12 7-inch waffles

Ingredients
For each variation, use 5 cups waffle batter or amount of batter from 1 pound dry waffle mix prepared according to package directions.
Blueberry Waffles: Add 1 cup fresh or frozen blueberries.
Cheese Waffles: Add 1/4 cup (2 ounces) shredded cheddar cheese.
Chocolate-Nut Waffles: Add 1 ounce melted unsweetened chocolate, 2 tablespoons sugar, 2 tablespoons chopped nuts.
Coconut Waffles: Add 1 cup finely chopped coconut and a drop of almond extract.
Corn Waffles: Add 1-1/2 cups well-drained whole kernel corn.
Date-Nut Waffles: Add 1/4 cup finely cut dates and 1/2 cup chopped nuts.
Ham or Bacon Waffles: Add 1 cup chopped ham or crumbled crisp bacon.
Mincemeat Waffles: Add 1 cup mincemeat.
Orange Waffles: Add grated rind from 1 large orange.
Peanut Butter Waffles: Add 1/3 cup creamy type peanut butter.
Pecan Waffles: Add 1 cup chopped pecans. (Add 2 teaspoons maple flavoring for Maple Pecan variation.)
Raisin-Nut Waffles: Add 1/4 cup washed, drained raisins and 1/2 cup chopped nuts.

CINNAMON PEAR CRESTED WAFFLES WITH CINNAMON SYRUP ⟶

Yield: 24 portions, 1 waffle, 2 pear halves, 1/3 cup syrup

Ingredients

BARTLETT PEARS, medium	1 No. 10 can
PEAR SYRUP AND WATER	1-1/2 quarts
SUGAR	1 quart
RED FOOD COLORING	12 drops (approx.)
CINNAMON EXTRACT	2 teaspoons
WAFFLES, freshly baked	24
WHIPPED CREAM	as desired

SHERRIED SHRIMP ON WAFFLES

Yield: 32 portions

Ingredients

SHRIMP, cooked, deveined*	2 pounds
SHERRY WINE	1 cup
CREAM OF MUSHROOM SOUP	1 50-ounce can
CHEDDAR CHEESE SOUP	1 50-ounce can
WAFFLES, FROZEN, toasted	64
PARSLEY SPRIGS	32

Procedure

1. Soak shrimp in sherry for at least 2 hours.
2. Combine soups; heat to simmer. Add shrimp and sherry. Heat through.
3. To serve, ladle 4 ounces (1/2 cup) over 2 hot waffles.

*or crab meat or lobster.

Procedure

1. Drain pears. Combine pear syrup and water and sugar, heat and stir until dissolved. Bring to a boil; boil slowly about 1 minute.
2. Remove from heat. Add red food coloring and cinnamon extract. (Ground cinnamon produces a cloudy syrup.)
3. Pour syrup over pears allowing sufficient syrup to cover fruit. Let stand about 1 hour or until pears are of the desired color.
4. To serve, cut pear halves in two, lengthwise. Arrange four pieces of pear on top of waffle. Garnish with whipped cream. Serve with a small pitcher of cinnamon syrup on the side.

FILBERT WAFFLES

Yield: 1-1/2 gallons batter, 48 portions

Ingredients

FLOUR	3 pounds
BAKING POWDER	6 tablespoons
SALT	2 tablespoons
SUGAR	4 ounces
FILBERTS, finely chopped	6 ounces
EGG YOLKS, beaten	1-1/2 cups (18)
MILK	2-1/4 quarts
BUTTER or SHORTENING, melted	1 pound
EGG WHITES, stiffly beaten	2-1/4 cups (18)

Procedure

1. Combine flour, baking powder, salt and sugar; sift. Add chopped nuts.
2. Combine beaten egg yolks and milk. Add to flour mixture; blend.
3. Lightly mix in melted butter.
4. Fold in beaten egg whites. Bake in a hot waffle iron.
5. Serve with butter and syrup; whipped cream and strawberries or peaches; or, creamed chicken or seafood.

WAFFLES WITH RED RED APPLE TOPPING

Yield: 24 portions

Ingredients
STRAWBERRIES, FROZEN, SWEETENED, thawed	1 No. 10 can (3 quarts)
APPLE PIE FILLING	1 No. 10 can
WAFFLES, FROZEN, toasted	48
WHIPPED CREAM or TOPPING, or WHIPPED CREAM CHEESE or SOUR CREAM	as needed

Procedure

1. Combine strawberries and pie filling.
2. Ladle 4 ounces (1/2 cup) over two hot waffles. Garnish with whipped cream, whipped topping, whipped cream cheese or sour cream.

CHERRIES JUBILEE WAFFLES

Yield: 24 portions

Ingredients
DARK SWEET CHERRIES, canned, pitted	3 quarts
SYRUP FROM CHERRIES	1 quart
SUGAR	1 cup
CINNAMON	1 teaspoon
MACE	1 teaspoon
CORNSTARCH	1/3 cup
WATER, cold	1/2 cup
KIRSCH	1/2 cup
WAFFLES, baked, hot	24

Procedure

1. Measure drained cherries, set aside.
2. Combine syrup, sugar and spices; bring to a boil.
3. Blend cornstarch with cold water. Stir into hot syrup; cook and stir until thickened and clear.
4. Add cherries; heat through. Remove from heat; add kirsch.
5. Serve warm sauce over waffles.

FRITTERS

Fritters Crisp from the Fryer

National Cherry Growers and Industries Foundation

APPLE FRITTERS

Yield: 50 portions, 2 fritters, No. 24 scoop

Ingredients

FLOUR	3 pounds
BAKING POWDER	1/2 cup
SALT	1 tablespoon
SUGAR	3/4 cup
NUTMEG	3/4 teaspoon
CINNAMON	1-1/2 teaspoons
APPLES, peeled, finely chopped	1-1/2 quarts
EGGS, beaten	12
MILK, WHOLE	1-1/2 quarts
SHORTENING, melted	1/3 cup

Procedure

1. Sift together flour, baking powder, salt, sugar and spices.
2. Add apples to dry ingredients; mix well.
3. Combine eggs and milk; add to flour mixture. Add shortening; mix until flour is dampened.
4. Drop in deep fat at 375°F. using a No. 24 scoop. Fry until golden brown. Drain; serve hot with syrup.

Corn Fritters and Canadian Bacon

Armour and Company

HAM AND CORN FRITTERS

Yield: 48 small fritters

Ingredients

FLOUR, sifted	1 quart (1 pound)
SALT	2 teaspoons
BAKING POWDER	4 teaspoons
EGGS, whole	8
MILK	2 cups
SALAD OIL	4 teaspoons
CORN, canned whole kernel, drained	1 quart
HAM or LUNCHEON MEAT, ground	1 quart

Procedure
1. Sift together flour, salt and baking powder.
2. Beat eggs; combine with milk. Add to flour mixture. Add salad oil; mix until all flour is dampened.
3. Fold in drained corn and ground ham.
4. Drop batter by spoonsful into deep fat heated to 375°F. Fry until brown, turning once. Drain on brown paper.

PRUNE FRITTERS ⟶

Yield: approximately 45 portions, 4 fritters each

Ingredients

PRUNES, WHOLE (40/50)	4 pounds
WATER, cold	as needed
EGGS, whole	1 pound
MILK	2 cups
COOKING OIL	1/4 cup
FLOUR, ALL-PURPOSE	1 pound
BAKING POWDER	2 tablespoons
SUGAR	1/4 cup
NUTMEG	1 teaspoon
SALT	1 tablespoon

CORN FRITTERS

Yield: 7 dozen

Ingredients

FLOUR	2 pounds
SUGAR	3-1/4 ounces
SALT	3/4 ounce
BAKING POWDER	3-1/4 ounces
EGGS, slightly beaten	6
MILK	3-1/4 cups
MARGARINE, melted	3-1/4 ounces
CORN, whole kernel, drained	1 pound, 12 ounces

Procedure

1. Combine flour, sugar, salt and baking powder; mix thoroughly.

2. Combine eggs, milk and margarine. Add to dry ingredients; beat until smooth. Add corn; mix thoroughly.

3. Dip 1-1/4 ounces batter for each fritter, using No. 30 scoop. Fry in deep fat at $360°$ to $375°F$. Turn to brown evenly.

4. Serve with syrup.

Procedure

1. Cover prunes with cold water. Allow to soak, at room temperature, 24 hours.
2. Bring to boil; simmer 3 to 5 minutes. Cool.
3. Drain. Remove pits, being careful to leave fruit whole. Dry on absorbent paper.
4. Beat eggs until light; add milk and oil.
5. Combine flour, baking powder, sugar, nutmeg and salt. Sift.
6. Combine dry ingredients with egg mixture; blend well.
7. Dip prunes in batter, coating well.
8. Fry in deep fat at 375°F. 2 to 3 minutes or until golden brown.
9. Serve hot with lemon sauce, brandy sauce, or other sauce, as desired.

CHERRY FRITTERS

Yield: 50 portions

Ingredients

FLOUR, ALL-PURPOSE	3-1/2 pounds
SUGAR, GRANULATED	1/2 cup
BAKING POWDER	1/4 cup
SALT	2 teaspoons
MILK	1 quart
EGGS, well-beaten	8
COOKING OIL	1/2 cup
MARASCHINO CHERRIES, halved, well-drained	3 quarts
SUGAR, CONFECTIONERS'	as needed

Procedure

1. Combine flour, sugar, baking powder and salt. Sift.
2. Combine milk, eggs and oil. Gradually add to dry ingredients; blend.
3. Fold in cherries.
4. Drop by tablespoonsful into deep fat at 375°F. Fry 3 to 5 minutes or until golden brown. Drain; dust with confectioners' sugar.

French Toast with Walnut Syrup

The Quaker Oats Company

FRENCH TOAST

MAKE IT plain, fancy, savory or sweet—French toast in any form finds high favor and boosts tabs at breakfast time and brunch. With a few simple tricks you can step up the appeal of this year 'round favorite by introducing variety and new presentations.

Try offering a flavored French toast. Or, the familiar plain version with an unusual accompaniment. Discover the number of interesting changes possible with a change of bread, a slight variation in method, or through the different types of equipment you can use.

The tang of orange juice zipped with a little of the grated rind brings a new flavor note to French toast. So does a mixture of cinnamon, sugar and nuts, or grated Parmesan cheese.

French toast can be fried in deep fat; it can be sauteed, grilled or baked. Each method results in a slightly different effect. Your choice of method or equipment may depend in part upon your particular serving needs. Make it on a griddle or in the fryer for quick cooked-to-order service. Use a waffle baker for gaining a special effect. Remember the advantages of the oven when preparing quantities for a crowd.

BREAD VARIATIONS
  Whole or half-slice triangles of white or raisin bread
  Diagonally-cut slices of French bread
  Slices of the twisted egg bread known as challah
  Slices of cheddar cheese bread

FLAVOR VARIATIONS
  Use buttermilk in place of sweet milk
  Substitute cream for milk; add a splash of sherry
  Add curry powder, mustard or grated cheese to the egg and milk mixture

VARIED PRESENTATION
  Sprinkle with confectioners' sugar or cinnamon sugar
  Garnish with sauteed apple rings
  Serve with plain, buttered or fruited syrup
  Serve with jelly, jam, marmalade, honey or spiced applesauce
  Serve with a sweet, flavored butter tasting of honey, maple syrup, orange rind, cinnamon or strawberries

BRUNCH FEATURES
  Deviled ham French toast topped with poached eggs
  French toast with creamed chipped beef or creamed ham
  Curried French toast with creamed chicken or seafood
  Cheese French toast with broiled tomatoes
  Orange French toast topped with sweetened orange sections
  Mustard-flavored French toast with grilled ham or Canadian bacon
  French toast slices with warm red cherry or blueberry sauce or sweetened crushed strawberries
  French toast sandwiched with ripe banana slices; warm syrup served on the side

CINNAMON ORANGE FRENCH TOAST

Yield: 48 portions

Ingredients

EGGS, beaten	3 pounds
SUGAR, CONFECTIONERS'	1/2 pound
ORANGE JUICE*	2 quarts
ORANGE RIND, grated (optional)	1/2 cup
ENRICHED BREAD, FRESH	96 slices
CINNAMON	1 tablespoon
SUGAR, GRANULATED	1/2 cup

Procedure
1. Combine beaten eggs, confectioners' sugar, orange juice and rind.
2. Dip bread in egg-orange mix.
3. Arrange each 24 slices in well-buttered bun pan.
4. Combine cinnamon and sugar; sprinkle on each slice.
5. Toast in oven at 500°F. until brown. Serve with honey, if desired.

*If concentrate, dilute by one-half usual amount.

DEEP FRIED FRENCH TOAST

Yield: 40 portions

Ingredients

FLOUR	1-1/4 pounds
BAKING POWDER	2 tablespoons
SALT	2 tablespoons
EGGS, beaten	2 pounds
MILK	2-1/2 quarts
ENRICHED BREAD, FRESH	80 slices

Procedure
1. Sift flour, baking powder and salt together.
2. Gradually add flour mixture to beaten eggs, beating constantly.
3. Add milk; blend.
4. Dip two slices bread and place in fryer basket; place another basket on top (prevents need for turning).
5. Fry in 375°F. fat until brown.

BREAKFAST AND BRUNCH DISHES

OVEN FRENCH TOAST ⟶

Yield: 48 portions, 2 slices each

Ingredients
EGGS, beaten	3/4 quart (1-1/2 pounds)
SALT	4 teaspoons
SUGAR	1 cup
MILK	2 quarts
ALMOND EXTRACT	4 teaspoons
ENRICHED BREAD, FRESH	96 slices

FLUFFY PARMESAN FRENCH TOAST

Yield: 48 portions

Ingredients
MILK	1 gallon
EGGS, beaten	3 pounds
FLOUR	1 pound, 5 ounces
SALT	2-1/2 tablespoons
BAKING POWDER	2-1/2 tablespoons
PARMESAN CHEESE, grated	1 pound
ENRICHED BREAD, FRESH	96 slices

Procedure
1. Put 2-1/2 quarts milk into shallow pan.
2. Combine remaining milk, eggs, flour, salt and baking powder in another pan. Beat until smooth; stir in cheese.
3. Dip bread in milk, then in egg-cheese mixture.
4. Brown on greased griddle (350°F.). Cover to insure puffing.

Procedure
1. Combine beaten eggs, salt, sugar, milk and almond extract.
2. Dip each bread slice in egg and milk mixture.
3. Arrange 24 slices on each well-greased 18-inch by 26-inch bun pan.
4. Toast in oven at 500°F. for approximately 10 minutes, or until golden brown.*
5. Serve hot with honey, sugar, preserves or maple syrup.

*It will not be necessary to turn toast if pans are placed on oven deck only. Dark or dull finish pans shorten baking time. Toast may be prepared in advance and reheated on order by returning to oven preheated to 450°F. for 5 minutes.

CINNAMON-NUT FRENCH TOAST

Yield: 48 portions

Ingredients
CINNAMON	1 cup
SUGAR	2-1/2 cups
PECANS or WALNUTS, chopped	1-1/2 quarts
EGGS, slightly beaten	2 pounds
MILK	2 quarts
ENRICHED BREAD, FRESH	96 slices

Procedure
1. Combine cinnamon, sugar, nuts.
2. Combine eggs and milk in shallow pan.
3. Dip slices in egg mix. Coat both sides.
4. Place in preheated waffle baker. Sprinkle tablespoon cinnamon-nut mix on each slice; close baker and brown.
5. Serve with honey or marmalade.

DEVILED HAM FRENCH TOAST

Yield: 45 portions

Ingredients
EGGS, beaten	1-1/2 pounds
MILK	2 quarts
DEVILED HAM	3 pounds
ENRICHED BREAD, FRESH	90 slices

Procedure
1. Combine eggs and milk in shallow pan.
2. Spread one tablespoon deviled ham over one side each slice of bread.
3. Dip slices into egg mixture. Coat both sides.
4. Place on well-greased, medium hot griddle (375°F.), ham side down. Grill until brown; turn.

GRILLED CUSTARD FRENCH TOAST

Yield: 48 portions

Ingredients
EGGS, beaten	6 pounds
MILK	2 quarts
SUGAR	2 pounds
SALT	1/3 cup
ENRICHED BREAD, FRESH	96 slices

Procedure
1. Combine beaten eggs, milk, sugar and salt in shallow pan.
2. Dip slices in egg mix. Coat both sides.
3. Place on well-greased hot griddle or waffle baker. Grill on both sides until brown.
4. Serve with honey, cinnamon-sugar, jam, jelly, fruit sauce or syrup.

FRENCH TOAST WITH STRAWBERRY BUTTER

Yield: 20 portions

Ingredients

STRAWBERRIES, FROZEN, SLICED	1 pound
SYRUP, reserved from strawberries	1/2 cup
BUTTER or MARGARINE, soft	6 ounces
SUGAR, CONFECTIONERS'	3 tablespoons
EGGS, slightly beaten	5
SUGAR, GRANULATED	1 tablespoon
VANILLA	3/4 teaspoon
MILK	1/2 cup
BREAD, WHITE, DAY-OLD	40 slices
CORN FLAKE CRUMBS	2-1/2 cups

Procedure

1. Drain strawberries. Measure required amount of syrup; set aside.
2. Whip butter until light and fluffy. Add confectioners' sugar gradually, beating thoroughly.
3. Heat strawberries (with remaining syrup) until slightly warm. Add to butter mixture gradually, beating thoroughly. Chill until ready to use.
4. Combine eggs, sugar and vanilla; beat well. Add milk and measured amount of strawberry syrup.
5. Dip bread slices in egg mixture; moisten thoroughly, turning once. Coat both sides with corn flake crumbs.
6. Brown bread slices in small amount of heated shortening. Serve at once with strawberry butter.

SYRUPS

Syrup Stars as Scrapple Topping

BROWNED SUGAR GINGER SYRUP

Yield: approximately 1 quart

Ingredients

SUGAR	2 cups
WATER, boiling	1 quart
SALT	1/2 teaspoon
BUTTER or MARGARINE	1-1/2 tablespoons
VANILLA EXTRACT	2 teaspoons
CORNSTARCH	1/4 cup
GINGER, GROUND	2 teaspoons
WATER, cold	2 to 3 tablespoons

Procedure

1. Heat sugar in a heavy pan over moderate heat, stirring constantly, until just melted.
2. Add boiling water and salt; reduce heat.
3. Add butter and vanilla; cook over low heat, stirring constantly, until smooth.
4. Mix cornstarch and ginger with cold water to form a thin smooth paste. Add to pan; cook and stir until blended and sauce is thickened.
5. Serve with pancakes, waffles or French toast.

CRANBERRY SYRUP

Yield: 1-1/2 gallons

Ingredients

CORNSTARCH	2-1/4 ounces
LEMON JUICE	1/2 cup
CRANBERRY JUICE	1 gallon
MAPLE SYRUP (IMITATION)	2 quarts

Procedure

1. Blend cornstarch and lemon juice. Stir in cranberry juice and maple syrup. Cook and stir until clear. Mixture will be thin.
2. Cool. Refrigerate. (Mixture will thicken to syrup consistency.)

SPICED BING CHERRY SAUCE

Yield: approximately 1 quart

Ingredients

BING CHERRIES, CANNED	1 quart
CORNSTARCH	2 tablespoons
SALT	1/4 teaspoon
CLOVES, GROUND	1/4 teaspoon
CINNAMON, GROUND	1 teaspoon
LEMON JUICE, FRESH	2 tablespoons
VANILLA EXTRACT	1 teaspoon

Procedure

    1. Drain cherries. Combine syrup with cornstarch, salt and spices; blend well.

    2. Cook and stir over low heat until slightly thickened. Add cherries, lemon juice and vanilla.

    3. Serve with pancakes, waffles or French toast.

STRAWBERRY BUTTER

Yield: 3 quarts

Ingredients

BUTTER or MARGARINE	2 pounds
SUGAR, CONFECTIONERS', sifted	3-1/2 pounds
VANILLA or BRANDY EXTRACT	1-1/2 tablespoons
STRAWBERRIES, FROZEN, SLICED, thawed, drained	5 pounds

Procedure

    1. Cream butter; gradually add sugar. Whip until fluffy.

    2. Blend in flavoring and drained strawberries. Chill several hours.

Note

    Use syrup drained from berries for sauces, fruit punches, gelatin desserts, etc.

BUTTERED PINEAPPLE PANCAKE SAUCE

Yield: approximately 2-1/2 quarts

Ingredients
BUTTER	12 ounces
PINEAPPLE, CANNED, CRUSHED (with syrup)	2 quarts
SUGAR, BROWN (packed measure)	1 cup (6 ounces)
NUTMEG, GROUND	1/2 teaspoon

Procedure
1. Melt butter; add remaining ingredients.
2. Simmer and stir until slightly thickened. Serve with corn meal pancakes.

SPICED PEACH AND RAISIN SAUCE

Yield: approximately 1-1/2 quarts

Ingredients
SUGAR	1 cup
CORNSTARCH	1/4 cup
SYRUP FROM CANNED PEACHES	1 quart
SALT	1/4 teaspoon
LEMON JUICE, FRESH	1/4 cup
BUTTER or MARGARINE	1/4 cup
PEACHES, CANNED, coarsely chopped	1 quart
RAISINS	1 cup
CINNAMON, GROUND	2 teaspoons
CLOVES, GROUND	1/2 teaspoon
LEMON RIND, grated	1 teaspoon

Procedure
1. Combine sugar and cornstarch; add peach syrup and salt, blending well.
2. Cook and stir over low heat until slightly thickened.
3. Add lemon juice, butter, peaches, raisins and spices. Bring to boiling point; remove from heat. Add lemon rind.
4. Serve with pancakes, waffles or French toast.

APPLE SYRUP PANCAKE SAUCE

Yield: 2 quarts

Ingredients

MAPLE SYRUP (IMITATION)	1-1/2 quarts
SALT	1/2 teaspoon
APPLES, peeled, finely chopped	1-1/2 pounds (3-1/2 cups)

Procedure
1. Combine syrup, salt and apples.
2. Simmer about 10 minutes. Serve warm or cold.

Variation
Decrease apples to 2 cups. Add 1-1/2 cups raisins.

HOT SPICED HONEY

Yield: 1 quart

Ingredients

BUTTER or MARGARINE	1 pound
CINNAMON	1 teaspoon
NUTMEG	1/2 teaspoon
HONEY	2 cups

Procedure
1. Melt butter; add spices.
2. Gradually add honey, beating constantly until well blended.
3. Heat before serving.

CINNAMON HONEY BUTTER

Yield: 1 quart

Ingredients

CINNAMON, GROUND	3 tablespoons
BUTTER or MARGARINE, softened	1-1/4 pounds
HONEY	1-1/2 cups

Procedure
1. Blend cinnamon with butter.
2. Add honey gradually, mixing until blended.

CHERRY PANCAKE SAUCE

Yield: 2 quarts

Ingredients

MAPLE SYRUP (IMITATION)	1 quart
SALT	1/2 teaspoon
CHERRIES, FROZEN, ground (with juice)	2 quarts (2-1/4 pounds)

Procedure
1. Heat syrup to boiling.
2. Remove from heat; add salt and ground cherries.
3. Serve warm or cold.

ORANGE HONEY BUTTER

Yield: 2-1/2 pounds

Ingredients

BUTTER	1 pound
HONEY	2 cups
ORANGE JUICE	1 tablespoon
ORANGE RIND, grated	1 to 2 tablespoons

Procedure
1. Beat butter until well creamed.
2. Add honey very gradually, continuing to beat.
3. Add orange juice slowly. Add orange rind; beat thoroughly.
4. Place in refrigerator to firm.
5. Serve with hot biscuits, pancakes, waffles or scones.

90 BREAKFAST AND BRUNCH DISHES

Eggs, Scrambled or Souffled

General Foods Corp.

Pillsbury Co.

EGG DISHES

EGGS FIT IN with every breakfast pattern. Prepared in various ways, they belong in the quick breakfast, the average time breakfast and the leisurely, hearty brunch.

Bacon and eggs are a standby, day in and day out. Add interest to poached or fried eggs with a bit of seasoned salt, a dash of paprika, a flutter of chopped parsley or a sprig of cress. Dress up scrambled eggs with chopped parsley, chives or herbs. Add mushrooms, chicken livers, bacon bits or minced ham. Or, add cheese in the form of cubed cream cheese, shredded cheddar, grated Parmesan or creamed cottage cheese. Serve plain scrambled eggs with creamed mushrooms, asparagus, ham or chipped beef.

For other special attractions, feature Eggs Benedict, Eggs Florentine, a Fresh Mushroom Quiche or a well-rounded-up golden omelet in fancy dress.

TOMATO-EGG SCRAMBLE

Yield: 48 portions

Ingredients

CREAM OF TOMATO SOUP, CONDENSED	2 50 or 51-ounce cans
PROCESS AMERICAN CHEESE, grated	3 pounds
EGGS, whole	1 gallon
SALT	1-1/2 tablespoons
MILK	3 cups
ENRICHED BREAD TOAST, buttered	48 slices
BACON, cooked (optional)	96 slices
PARSLEY SPRIGS	48

Procedure

1. Combine undiluted soup and grated cheese in top of a double boiler. Place over boiling water; heat, stirring occasionally, until cheese melts and blends evenly into soup.

2. Beat eggs slightly; add salt and milk; blend. Scramble just before serving time.

3. For each portion, ladle 1/3 cup of the tomato-cheese sauce over a No. 8 scoop of scrambled eggs. Cut a slice of buttered toast across diagonally. Arrange on the plate with two bacon strips, if desired. Garnish with parsley.

Scrambled Eggs au Gratin

Poultry and Egg National Board

VILLAGE HAM 'N EGGS

Yield: 48 portions

Ingredients

HAM, cooked	5 pounds
BUTTER or MARGARINE	12 ounces
FLOUR	2 cups
MILK, heated	1 gallon
PROCESS CHEESE, CHEDDAR, grated	1-1/2 pounds
SALT	2 teaspoons
PEPPER	1 teaspoon
PIMIENTOS, diced	3/4 cup
EGGS, hard-cooked, diced	24
ENGLISH MUFFINS, split, toasted	48

Procedure

1. Cut ham in julienne strips.
2. Melt butter; blend in flour.
3. Add hot milk and grated cheese. Cook and stir over medium heat until sauce is thick and smooth.
4. Add seasonings, pimientos, ham and eggs.
5. Serve hot over toasted muffins.

SHIRRED EGGS BRETONNE ⟶

Yield: 24 portions

Ingredients

BUTTER or MARGARINE	1/4 pound
ONION, minced	1/2 cup
MUSHROOMS, chopped	2 cups
SALT	1/2 teaspoon
PEPPER (optional)	1/8 teaspoon
EGGS	24
NON-FAT DRY MILK	2 tablespoons
WATER	1/2 cup

INDIVIDUAL CASSEROLE OF BAKED SPINACH AND EGGS

Yield: 15 portions

Ingredients

SPINACH, frozen	2 2-pound packages
CREAM OF MUSHROOM SOUP	1 51-ounce can
EGGS	30
SALT	as needed
PEPPER	as needed

Procedure

1. Cook spinach in boiling salted water. Drain thoroughly. Mix with undiluted soup.

2. Divide mixture into 15 casseroles. With back of spoon, make two nests in the spinach in each casserole. Break an egg into each indentation. Sprinkle lightly with salt and pepper.

3. Bake in oven at 375°F. for 15 to 20 minutes or until eggs are set.

Procedure

1. Melt butter in a large skillet. Add onions and mushrooms; saute until tender. Add salt and pepper.

2. Spoon about 2-1/2 teaspoons mushroom mixture into each of 24 5-ounce custard cups. Rub mixture around inside of custard cups with a small spatula to grease them.

3. Break one egg into each cup.

4. Sift dry milk over water; stir until dissolved.

5. Put 1 teaspoon milk over top of each egg.

6. Place custard cups into shallow baking pans. Bake in oven at 325°F. for 20 minutes or until done. Serve at once.

Note

Bake with or without water bath.

EGGS FLORENTINE

Yield: 25 portions

Ingredients

SPINACH, frozen	4-1/2 pounds
BUTTER or MARGARINE	3 ounces
SALT	as needed
PEPPER	as needed
MONOSODIUM GLUTAMATE	as needed
EGGS	50
HOLLANDAISE SAUCE	1-1/2 quarts

Procedure

1. Cook spinach according to package directions. Add butter and seasonings.

2. To serve: place 3 ounces spinach in individual oval casseroles. Poach two eggs per order; place on hot spinach. Mask eggs with hollandaise. Run under broiler a few seconds, if desired.

Eggs Benedict

Armour and Company

EGGS BENEDICT

Yield: 24 portions (1 egg, 2 slices bacon and one muffin)

Ingredients	
CANADIAN BACON, sliced 1/4 inch thick	48 1-1/2 ounce slices
ENGLISH MUFFINS, split and toasted	24
EGGS, poached	24
SHERRY HOLLANDAISE SAUCE*	4-1/2 cups

Procedure
1. Trim all fat from bacon; grill until edges curl.
2. Place a bacon slice on each half of toasted muffin.
3. Top half of each muffin with a poached egg. Cut remaining bacon-topped muffins in two; arrange one half at each side of egg-topped muffins.
4. Spoon 3 tablespoons sherry hollandaise sauce over each portion.

*See recipe facing page.

Note
If preferred, cut bacon 1/8-inch thick; use 96 slices and allow 4 per portion.

*SHERRY HOLLANDAISE SAUCE

Yield: 3-1/3 cups, 24 1-ounce portions

Ingredients

BUTTER	1 pound
LEMON JUICE	1/4 cup
EGG YOLKS	3/4 cup
SALT	1/4 teaspoon
CAYENNE PEPPER	1/8 teaspoon
PAPRIKA	1/8 teaspoon
SHERRY	1/4 cup
WATER, hot	1/4 cup

Procedure

1. Melt half of the butter over low heat, or in the top of a double boiler over hot water. Add lemon juice and egg yolks. Cook slowly, beating constantly.

2. Add half (1/4 pound) of remaining butter; after it melts, add rest of butter. Stir until it melts. Add salt, pepper and paprika.

3. When thick, remove from heat. Heat sherry, blend in quickly, beating constantly.

4. If mixture starts to separate, quickly add hot water; stir sauce vigorously.

Note

To reheat sauce: place in top of double boiler over hot water; add 1/3 cup hot water; beat vigorously until blended smoothly.

EGGS BENEDICT

Yield: 14 portions

Ingredients

CREAM OF CELERY SOUP, CONDENSED	1 50-ounce can
MAYONNAISE	1-1/4 cups
LEMON JUICE	2 tablespoons
ENGLISH MUFFINS	14
HAM SLICES, thin, lightly grilled	28
EGGS, poached	28

Procedure

1. Blend soup, mayonnaise and lemon juice; heat slowly. (If a thinner sauce is desired, blend in a small amount of water.)
2. Split English muffins; toast.
3. Arrange a slice of ham on each toasted muffin half. Top with a poached egg. Serve two halves with 1/2 cup sauce. Garnish with a sprinkle of paprika.

GOURMET SCRAMBLE

Yield: 1 portion (cooked to order)

Ingredients

EGG, well beaten	1
MILK	2 tablespoons
SALTINE CRACKERS, crumbled	10 (about 2/3 cup)

Procedure

1. Combine ingredients, let stand 5 minutes.
2. Fry in small frying pan with a generous amount of butter or margarine. Turn once.
3. Serve with syrup, jelly or sprinkled with sugar and cinnamon.

FRESH MUSHROOM QUICHE

Yield: 4 9-inch

Ingredients

BACON, sliced	1 pound
BACON FAT	3/4 cup
ONION, finely chopped	1-1/3 cups
MUSHROOMS, coarsely chopped	2 pounds
FLOUR	1/4 cup
EGGS, lightly beaten	16
CREAM, HEAVY	1 quart
MILK	3 cups
SALT	2 teaspoons
BLACK PEPPER, ground	1/2 teaspoon
NUTMEG, ground	3/4 teaspoon
PASTRY SHELLS, 9-inch, unbaked	4
GRUYERE CHEESE, grated	1 pound
MUSHROOM CAPS, whole, broiled	as needed

Procedure

1. Cook bacon until crisp. Drain. Crumble. Measure required amount of bacon fat.
2. Saute onion in bacon fat until limp. Add chopped mushrooms; saute until tender, adding more bacon fat, if necessary. Blend in flour. Cool mixture a few minutes.
3. Combine eggs, cream, milk and seasonings.
4. Sprinkle crumbled bacon over bottom of pastry shells. Top with grated cheese. Spread with mushroom mixture. Pour egg mixture over all.
5. Bake in oven at 425°F. for 15 minutes. Reduce heat to 300°F.; bake 40 minutes longer or until custard is set.
6. Serve warm, garnished with broiled mushroom caps.

EGG CROQUETTES AND CELERY SAUCE

Yield: 48 portions

Ingredients

EGGS, hard-cooked	48
BREAD CRUMBS, fine dry	6 cups
ONION, finely chopped	1 cup
SALT	1 tablespoon
PEPPER, black	dash
CREAM OF CELERY SOUP, CONDENSED	3 50-ounce cans
MILK	1 quart
PARSLEY, chopped	1/2 cup

Procedure

1. Shell eggs, sieve. Mix with 5 cups of the bread crumbs, the onion, seasonings and one can of the soup.

2. Shape into 96 small croquettes, using a No. 24 scoop. (For large croquettes, use No. 12 scoop.)

3. Roll croquettes in remaining crumbs.

4. Fry in deep fat at 350°F. for about 5 minutes or until golden brown.

5. Blend remaining soup with milk; add parsley. Heat. Serve over croquettes.

SCRAMBLED EGGS

Yield: 50 1/2-cup portions

Ingredients
EGGS	3 quarts
BUTTER, soft	6 ounces
WATER, cold	3/4 cup
SALT	1-1/2 tablespoons
PEPPER	1/2 to 1 teaspoon
WHITE SAUCE, medium	1 quart

Procedure
1. Beat eggs with butter, water, salt and pepper until light.
2. Heat lightly greased scrambling utensil until moderately hot.
3. Pour egg mixture into utensil; cook over moderate heat. As eggs thicken, lift with pancake turner.
4. While eggs are still quite soft, blend in white sauce. Continue cooking to desired doneness.
5. Serve promptly, avoid further cooking.

Note
If service is to be delayed, cook eggs to a less firm consistency. Cover pan and hold in oven at 200°F. Eggs may be held up to 1 hour.

HERB SCRAMBLED EGGS

Yield: 24 portions

Ingredients	
EGGS	1-1/4 quarts
SALT	1-1/2 teaspoons
PEPPER	1/8 teaspoon
MILK, WHOLE FLUID	3 cups
TARRAGON, dried, ground	1/4 teaspoon
MARJORAM, ground	1/4 teaspoon
SAVORY, ground	1/4 teaspoon
OREGANO, ground	1/4 teaspoon
BASIL, ground	1/4 teaspoon
BUTTER or MARGARINE	1/4 cup (2 ounces)

Procedure

1. Beat eggs slightly. Add salt, pepper, milk and herbs; blend thoroughly.

2. Cook to order, as needed, by following steps 3, 4, 5 and 6.

3. Melt 1/2 teaspoon butter in a shallow small omelet pan, tilting pan to grease bottom and sides.

4. When hot, pour in 1/3 cup of egg mixture; reduce heat.

5. Cook slowly, continually lifting mixture from bottom and sides with a spatula as it sets, so liquid can flow to bottom.

6. Avoid constant stirring. Cook until set and still moist.

Crisp Bacon Over Quiche

National Live Stock and Meat Board

OVEN SCRAMBLED EGGS AND CHEESE

Yield: 24 portions

Ingredients
EGGS	20 (1 quart)
MILK, hot	2-1/2 cups
SALT	2 teaspoons
CHEESE, grated	8 ounces (2 cups)
BUTTER or MARGARINE	4 ounces

Procedure

   1. Beat eggs slightly. Add milk and salt; mix well.

   2. Add cheese.

   3. Melt butter in a 16-inch by 10-inch by 2-inch pan. Add egg mixture.

   4. Bake in oven at 350°F. for 20 minutes; stir. Continue baking until cooked to desired doneness, about 20 minutes.

Dill Pickle Omelet
Chef John L. Kaufmann, Drake Hotel, Chicago

Pickle Packers International, Inc.

OMELETS

OMELET MAKING can be a scene stealer. In today's open kitchens or on a buffet, this simple but show-off bit of cookery is full of drama. People will always be fascinated by a cook's quick, sure movements in building a light, tender omelet before he quickly slides it from the pan.

Quite aside from showmanship, omelets are also valued for economy, quick preparation and their fabulous range. You can make an omelet sweet or have it savory; roll it up, fold it double, or serve it open-faced. You can ring a change with seasonings, add a tasty filling, or ladle on a sauce. What follows is just a sampling of what can be done with omelets.

SUGGESTIONS FOR ADDITIONS TO BEATEN EGGS (OR YOLKS)

- *A mixture of finely cut fresh herbs, such as chervil, parsley, chives and tarragon
- *Small croutons and/or grated cheese
- *Sauteed mushroom pieces
- *Sauteed minced green pepper, slivers of pimiento
- *Minced cooked ham, crisp bacon bits or frizzled finely cut chipped beef
- *Chopped parsley or watercress

FILLINGS

*Sauteed or creamed sliced mushrooms
*Hot buttered asparagus tips or sliced artichoke bottoms
*Well-seasoned chopped cooked spinach
*Hot fresh tomato pulp seasoned with onion and parsley
*Sauteed diced potatoes, herbs and chopped ham
*Potatoes sauteed in bacon fat, crumbled bacon
*Diced cooked shrimp, crab or lobster (cut small, heated in butter)
*Creamed flaked fish
*Sliced cooked sausages or crumbled bacon
*Ham (diced or chopped or cut in narrow strips)
*Corned beef hash
*Minced cooked kidney
*Creamed diced sweetbreads
*Sauteed chicken livers, coarsely diced
*Hot chopped chicken
*Grated sharp cheddar or Swiss cheese

FILLINGS FOR SWEET OMELETS

*Jam, jelly or marmalade (sprinkle top with confectioners' sugar)
*Apricot preserves, sauteed slivered almonds
*Crumbled marron glaces sprinkled with kirsch (glaze top with sugar, flame with kirsch, if desired)
*Mincemeat (flame with rum)
*Sliced fresh strawberries in stiffly whipped cream
*A blend of cottage and cream cheese flavored with grated orange rind. (Serve with crushed, sweetened strawberries)

SAUCES

*A la King
*Supreme
*Creamed shrimp or Creole shrimp
*Lobster Newburg
*Chicken a la King
*Cheese or Mornay sauce
*Asparagus and mushroom sauce
*Chicken livers in brown sauce
*Creamed chicken with peas
*Creamed sweetbreads and mushrooms
*Spanish, tomato, or Hong Kong sauce
*Cream sauce with onion or mushrooms (sprinkle sauced omelet with Parmesan, run under broiler)
*Cream sauce with sour cream, mushrooms and dill

PLAIN OMELET

Yield: 1 portion

Ingredients

EGGS	3
WATER, cold	1 tablespoon
SALT	1/8 teaspoon
PEPPER, WHITE	dash
BUTTER	1 tablespoon

Procedure

1. Break eggs into a bowl; add water, salt and pepper. Beat with a fork until whites and yolks are well mixed. Do not overbeat.

2. Heat omelet pan slowly until the butter sizzles at the touch. Melt butter in pan, stirring it around quickly to coat bottom of pan and sides.

3. Pour in eggs. Shake the pan back and forth with one hand, stirring the eggs in a circular motion (using the fork flat on bottom of pan) with the other.

4. When cooked but still soft on top,* hold handle with fingers of one hand, the palm turned upward. Tilt pan to a 45 degree angle; using fork, begin to roll omelet away from handle toward opposite side. Turn out onto a hot plate. Brush top with butter.

*Add filling, if used, at this point. Place on one-third of omelet, in the area next to the handle.

FRENCH OMELET ⟶

Yield: 5 omelets

Ingredients

EGGS	12
WATER	3 tablespoons
SALT	1/2 teaspoon
HOT PEPPER SAUCE	1/4 teaspoon
BUTTER	5 tablespoons
PARSLEY, chopped	5 teaspoons
BACON, cooked, crumbled	5 tablespoons

TWO EGG OMELET

Yield: 24 3/4-cup portions

Ingredients

MILK, WHOLE FLUID	2-1/4 quarts
SALT	2 teaspoons
PEPPER	1/4 teaspoon
EGGS	48
BUTTER or MARGARINE	1/2 pound

Procedure

1. Combine milk, salt and pepper with eggs, beating until well-blended.

2. For each order: Melt 2 teaspoons butter in individual small skillets or omelet pans.

3. When butter begins to bubble, tip pan slightly to grease sides as well as bottom of pan.

4. Add 3/4 cup of egg mixture; cook over low heat until mixture sets and lightly browns on the bottom.

5. Using a spatula, loosen omelet from edge of skillet, fold and roll out onto serving plate. Serve immediately.

Procedure

1. Break eggs into a large mixing bowl. Combine water, salt and hot pepper sauce; add to eggs. Beat with a rotary beater only until blended well; do not beat until frothy.

2. For each omelet, melt 1 tablespoon butter in pan. (Pan tests hot enough when drop of water spatters in pan.) Add 1 teaspoon parsley and 1 tablespoon bacon. Add 1/5 of the egg mixture (about 4 ounces).

3. Action is important, so is position of hands. Place left hand on pan handle with palm down. Move pan back and forth. Hold fork in right hand; move in circular motion with fork flat on bottom of pan, about 7 times. Omelet should be ready to be turned out.

4. Reverse position of left hand, placing it under handle with palm upward. Lift handle up; roll omelet away from handle with fork; turn out on hot plate.

Important: Do not wash pan; wipe clean with paper towel.

HONG KONG OMELET SAUCE

Yield: approx. 2-1/4 quarts

Ingredients

BUTTER or MARGARINE	1/4 pound
GREEN PEPPER, chopped	1/2 cup
ONION, chopped	1 cup
CORNSTARCH	1/4 cup
SALT	1 teaspoon
PEPPER	1/2 teaspoon
THYME	1 teaspoon
TOMATOES, canned	2 quarts
SOY SAUCE	1 to 2 tablespoons
ALMONDS, slivered, toasted	1 cup

Procedure

1. Melt butter; saute green pepper and onion until tender-crisp.

2. Blend in cornstarch and seasonings. Add tomatoes and soy sauce. Cook and stir until mixture thickens and comes to a boil. Add almonds.

3. Serve over individual plain or puffy omelets. Garnish with additional toasted slivered almonds, if desired.

SPANISH OMELET →

Yield: 50 portions

Ingredients

SHORTENING	8 ounces
ONIONS, chopped	12 ounces
GREEN PEPPERS, chopped	12 ounces
MUSHROOMS, chopped	1 pound
TOMATOES	1/2 No. 10 can
TOMATO PASTE	2 cups
STOCK or WATER	1 quart
FLOUR	2 tablespoons
BUTTER or MARGARINE, melted	2 ounces
SALT	2 tablespoons
PEPPER	1 tablespoon
PARSLEY, chopped	1/2 cup
GARLIC, chopped or	2 cloves
INSTANT GRANULATED GARLIC	1/4 teaspoon
OLIVES, STUFFED, chopped	2-1/2 cups
EGGS, beaten	7-3/4 pounds (3-7/8 quarts)
MILK	1 quart
SALT	1/4 cup

Procedure

1. Melt shortening; saute onions, peppers and mushrooms until tender, but not brown.

2. Add tomatoes, tomato paste and stock.

3. Combine flour and melted butter; stir until smooth. Add to tomato mixture. Bring to a boil; boil 2 minutes stirring constantly.

4. Add salt, pepper, parsley, garlic and olives; mix well. Reduce heat; simmer 5 minutes; keep hot.

5. Combine well-beaten eggs, milk and salt for omelets.

6. Pour egg mixture in 1/2 cup amounts on well-greased griddle; cook at moderate heat until golden brown on bottom. Fold each omelet over carefully; lift onto serving plate. Ladle Spanish sauce over omelet.

Note

To prepare 12 portion amount for cafeteria service, pour 1-1/2 quarts egg mixture on well-greased griddle; cook as above. Divide omelet in half lengthwise; fold one section over the other carefully with spatula; Cut into 12 portions; slide into hot counter pans; top with Spanish sauce.

MUSHROOM OMELET

Yield: 24 portions

Ingredients

OMELET
EGG YOLKS, beaten	48 (1 quart)
MILK	1-1/2 cups
CORNSTARCH	1/2 cup
BUTTER, melted	3/4 pound
SALT	2 to 3 teaspoons
EGG WHITES	48 (1-1/2 quarts)

SAUCE
MUSHROOMS, sliced	1-1/2 pounds
BUTTER	6 ounces
TOMATO SAUCE	1-1/2 quarts
CHEESE, PROCESSED CHEDDAR	1-1/2 pounds

Procedure

    1. Combine egg yolks, milk, cornstarch, butter and salt.

    2. Beat egg whites until they form stiff glossy peaks. Fold into yolk mixture.

    3. Pour into 12-inch by 20-inch by 2-inch pan. Bake in oven at 325°F. for 1 hour or until done.

    4. Saute mushrooms in butter. Stir in tomato sauce and cheese. Heat and stir until cheese melts and mixture is blended.

    5. Cut omelet in 3-inch squares. Serve with 1/3 cup sauce.

MOUSSELINE DESSERT OMELET

Yield: 2 portions

Ingredients

EGG YOLKS	4
SALT	1/8 teaspoon
SUGAR	2 tablespoons
CREAM, HEAVY	1 tablespoon
EGG WHITES	3
SUGAR	1 tablespoon
BUTTER	2-1/2 tablespoons
APRICOT PRESERVES	3 to 4 tablespoons
CONFECTIONERS' SUGAR	as needed

Procedure

1. Beat egg yolks with salt, first amount of sugar and cream until creamy and pale.
2. Beat whites with remaining sugar until glossy and stiff, not dry.
3. Combine mixtures until blended.
4. Heat omelet pan slowly. Melt butter, coating bottom and sides. When foaming subsides, pour in eggs. Stir with a spoon, pulling outer edges toward center. At the same time shake pan back and forth with other hand to prevent sticking. (Cook over lower heat than used for a plain omelet.)
5. Spoon preserves across top portion close to handle. Fold over (rather than rolling); slide out onto hot dish. Dust with confectioners' sugar.

Note

Flame omelet with brandy, if desired.

SHORT CAKES AND BENEDICT

Rapid Ready Rarebit in Puff Pastry

Pickle Packers International, Inc.

FRESH TOMATO SHORTCAKE

Yield: 24 portions

Ingredients
SHORTCAKE BISCUITS, hot	24
BUTTER	as needed
TOMATO SLICES, peeled, ripe	48
SALT	as needed
PEPPER	as needed
CHEESE SAUCE, hot	3 quarts
BACON STRIPS, cut in half, cooked	24 strips
OLIVES, STUFFED	24
PARSLEY, sprigs	24

Procedure

1. Split and butter shortcake biscuits. Place a tomato slice between each biscuit and on top, sprinkle tomato with salt and pepper, as desired.

2. Cover with cheese sauce; top each portion with two half strips of bacon. Garnish with olive and parsley.

ASPARAGUS BENEDICT

Yield: 1 portion

Ingredients
TOAST, trimmed	1 slice
HAM, baked	1 3-ounce slice
ASPARAGUS SPEARS, cooked	5
HOLLANDAISE SAUCE	1 ounce
PAPRIKA	to garnish
PARSLEY	to garnish
PARSIENNE POTATOES	6

Procedure

1. Place toast on plate; top with slice of ham. Arrange asparagus across ham.

2. Pour Hollandaise sauce over asparagus and sprinkle with a little paprika. Garnish with parsley and serve with Parsienne potatoes.

PLANTATION SHORTCAKE

Yield: 25 7-ounce portions

Ingredients

GREEN PEPPER, cut in strips	4 ounces
MUSHROOMS, sliced	8 ounces
PIMIENTO, cut in thin strips	4 ounces
BUTTER or MARGARINE	1 ounce
CREAM SAUCE, hot	4-1/2 quarts
TURKEY, cooked	1 pound
HAM, baked	1-1/2 pounds
CORN BREAD	25 squares

Procedure

1. Saute the green pepper, mushrooms and pimiento in the butter for 10 minutes. Add to the cream sauce.

2. Cut the turkey and the ham in julienne strips. Add to the sauce.

3. Split corn bread squares and toast under broiler until lightly browned.

4. To serve, put the halves of corn bread together again in shortcake fashion, with the creamed turkey and ham mixture between and over the top.

POTATO DISHES

Crisp Fried Potatoes Complete Popular Breakfast Plate

Poultry and Egg National Board

POTATO MUFFETS

Yield: approximately 50

Ingredients

MASHED POTATO GRANULES	1-1/2 pounds (3 cups)
WATER, boiling	1-1/2 quarts
SALT	1 tablespoon
BUTTER	1/4 pound
MILK, scalded	1 quart
EGGS	4

Procedure

1. Add dry potatoes gradually to boiling water and salt in mixing bowl. Whip at medium speed until well mixed, about 1 minute.

2. Mix in butter thoroughly. Add milk gradually and whip 2 minutes, or until light and fluffy. Whip at high speed 15 seconds. Add eggs gradually, beating to blend.

3. Fill paper or foil-lined muffin pans with the mixture using a No. 16 scoop. Or, drop onto a greased baking sheet. Make a slight hollow in top of each muffet with the back of the scoop. Brown in oven at 450°F. for about 10 minutes or until slightly browned.

4. Fill cavity with any of the following fillings:

    1/2 ounce grated Cheddar cheese

    1 slice crumbled crisp bacon

    1 tablespoon deviled ham

    1 tablespoon creamed peas with diced pimiento

    Return to oven for a few minutes.

Or add 1 tablespoon sour cream and chopped chives (serve this muffet immediately. Do not return to oven.)

POTATOES CONCORD

Yield: 24 1/2-cup portions

Ingredients

POTATOES, mashed, seasoned (hot or cold)	3 quarts (5-3/4 pounds)
MILK	2 tablespoons

Procedure

 1. Put thoroughly mashed potatoes into a pastry bag fitted with a rosette point.
 2. Squeeze potatoes through pastry bag to make 24 rosettes, 1/2-cup each.
 3. Brush each rosette with milk. Brown in oven at 450°F. for about 10 minutes.

SWEET POTATO BALLS

Yield: 24 portions (72 balls)

Ingredients

SWEET POTATOES, cooked, mashed	1-1/2 gallons (15 pounds raw weight)
PINEAPPLE CHUNKS, WATER PACKED, drained	72 pieces (2 No. 211 cans)

Procedure

 1. Season potatoes to taste.
 2. Form potato balls, using a No. 12 scoop. Drop balls onto a greased bun pan 18-inch by 26-inch by 1-inch.
 3. Press a pineapple chunk into center of each ball with a spatula. Use spatula to cover pineapple with potato.
 4. Bake in oven at 450°F. for 10 minutes, or until heated through.

POTATO PUFF BALLS

Yield: 18 puffs, 1/3 cup each

Ingredients

POTATOES, mashed, hot	1 quart
EGG YOLKS, beaten	4
PARSLEY, chopped	2 tablespoons
ONION, minced	1 teaspoon
SALT	1 teaspoon
EGG WHITES	4

Procedure

1. Blend mashed potatoes, egg yolks, parsley, onion and salt together thoroughly.
2. Beat the egg whites until stiff peaks form. Fold into potato mixture.
3. Spoon 1/3 cup mixture into well-greased muffin cups. Brush tops with melted butter.
4. Bake puffs in oven at 375°F. until lightly browned, about 30 to 35 minutes.

Potato Dishes 121

Pickle Piquancy for a Farmer's Breakfast

Pickle Packers International, Inc.

122 BREAKFAST AND BRUNCH DISHES

Many Forms, Flavors for Breakfast Breads

Pillsbury Food Service

BREADS

THE BREAD on your breakfast menu, if need be, can be limited to toast and still not become dull. There's the stand-by made with white bread which also serves as a basis for cinnamon toast and an offering of milk toast as well. Then there's whole wheat, cracked wheat, rye and raisin bread toast. There are toasted egg muffins, crumpets, corn bread squares, cinnamon buns and pecan rolls.

But why limit the breakfast bread to toast? Oven-hot biscuits, muffins, coffee cakes and freshly baked yeast rolls have become easy to schedule made from recipes that take advantage of time-saving methods: from mixes or with items that come ready to bake. Expand your breakfast bread offerings (1) with a selection of hot breads, or (2) concentrate on one item to feature as a specialty. Croissants, brioche, almond Danish, raisin scones, apple-nut muffins, blueberry kuchen, popovers, buttermilk biscuits, glazed orange rolls and gingerbread (served with butter) are only a sampling of the kitchen-baked items that you can bring into play to merchandise your breakfast menu.

Take Danish pastries, for example, made up in a variety of

styles but all in a miniature size. Serve, say, three of these small versions to an order instead of one of a regular size. Or, feature the small Danish on a more lavish scale, in a basket, perhaps, that is placed on each table. Or, pass them to patrons, inviting their selection from a well-arranged cart or tray.

Feathery Texture for Muffins

Pillsbury Co.

Muffins

MUFFINS are one of the best-known and versatile items in the quick bread roster. You can make them with novelty flours; add various flavorings; include sweet or savory ingredients; change them in countless exciting ways.

Corn muffins, one of the most popular variations, can be sweet or non-sweet, according to the prevailing taste. Then you can vary them further by baking the batter in different forms, as muffins, corn bread or corn sticks. For the well-browned crusty kinds, use a non-sweet batter and well-greased heavy pans. Rounds, baked an inch or more thick, command attention. Cut them in pie-shaped wedges and present them with honey or spicy apple butter as another pleasant change.

BASIC MUFFINS

Yield: 130 dozen

Ingredients

FLOUR, BREAD	27 pounds
FLOUR, PASTRY	9 pounds
SUGAR	13-1/2 pounds
NONFAT DRY MILK POWDER	3 pounds, 15 ounces
BAKING POWDER	1 pound, 14 ounces
SALT	5 ounces
SHORTENING, ALL VEGETABLE, HIGH EMULSIFYING	12 pounds
EGGS	9 pounds
WATER	31 pounds

Procedure

1. Scale dry ingredients and shortening in large mixer bowl. Mix 7 minutes, using pastry knife on second speed.

2. Mix eggs and water. Add to dry mixture; mix until smooth.

3. Fill muffin pans using No. 24 scoop. Bake in oven at 400°F. for 15 minutes.

Variations

Blueberry Muffins: add 3 gallons frozen blueberries. Sprinkle tops of unbaked muffins with cinnamon sugar.

Raisin Muffins: add 2-1/4 gallons raisins. Sprinkle tops of unbaked muffins with cinnamon sugar.

Orange Raisin Muffins: add 4-1/2 quarts coarsely ground oranges and 4-1/2 quarts raisins.

APPLE NUT MUFFINS

Yield: 14 dozen

Ingredients	
SUGAR, GRANULATED	2-1/2 pounds
SHORTENING	1-1/2 pounds
SUGAR, BROWN	1 pound
EGGS	12
FLOUR	4 pounds
SODA	1/2 ounce (4 teaspoons)
SALT	1 ounce (2 tablespoons)
MILK	2 pounds (1 quart)
APPLES (CANNED, SLICED) chopped	4-1/2 pounds
PECANS, chopped	2 quarts
SUGAR, GRANULATED	1-3/4 cups
CINNAMON	1 tablespoon

Procedure

1. Cream first amount of granulated sugar and shortening. Scrape down mixer paddle and bowl.

2. Add brown sugar and eggs; beat well.

3. Sift flour, soda and salt together. Add to sugar mixture alternately with milk. Add apples.

4. Fill greased muffin pans, using No. 16 scoop. Sprinkle tops with chopped pecans.

5. Mix remaining sugar and cinnamon. Sprinkle over pecan-topped batter.

6. Bake in oven at 350°F. for 30 minutes or until done. Serve warm with apple butter.

BLUEBERRY MUFFINS →

Yield: 8 dozen

Ingredients

FLOUR, ALL-PURPOSE	4 pounds, 2 ounces
NONFAT DRY MILK	1 pound
BAKING POWDER	6 ounces (1 cup)
SALT	1 ounce (2 tablespoons)
SHORTENING	13 ounces
SUGAR	14 ounces (2 cups)
EGGS, beaten	1 pound (2 cups)
WATER	2 quarts
BLUEBERRIES, well drained	1 quart

GOLDEN CORN MUFFINS

Yield: 100 medium muffins

Ingredients

YELLOW CORN MEAL	1-1/2 quarts
FLOUR, sifted	1-1/2 quarts
SUGAR	1 cup
SALT	1 tablespoon
BAKING POWDER	1/3 cup
EGGS, beaten	4
MILK	1-1/2 quarts
SHORTENING, soft	1-1/2 cups (12 ounces)

Procedure

1. Sift dry ingredients into mixer bowl. Add eggs, milk and shortening.

2. Start mixer at low speed; increase to medium speed; beat until batter is fairly smooth, about 1/2 minute. Do not overbeat.

3. Fill greased muffin pans 2/3 full. Bake in oven at 425°F. for about 20 minutes.

Variations

Corn Sticks: Bake in hot, greased corn stick pans 15 to 20 minutes.
Corn Bread: Bake in two greased 16-inch by 10-inch by 2-inch pans 20 to 25 minutes.

Procedure
1. Sift flour, dry milk, baking powder and salt together.
2. Cream shortening and sugar.
3. Add beaten eggs, one-third at a time, creaming well after each addition.
4. Add sifted dry ingredients to creamed mixture; then add all of water.
5. Mix until just combined. Add blueberries.
6. Fill well-greased muffin pans, using No. 20 scoop.
7. Bake in oven at 400°F. for 25 to 30 minutes.

RAISIN PEANUT FILLING

Yield: Filling for 80 muffins

Ingredients

PEANUT BUTTER, CHUNK STYLE	5 pounds, 6 ounces
SUGAR, GRANULATED or BROWN	1 pound
RAISINS, SEEDLESS	3 pounds
BUTTER or MARGARINE, melted	10 ounces

Procedure
1. Combine ingredients; blend. (If mixture is too stiff to swirl easily, heat over low heat or over hot water.)
2. To use, spoon about 1-3/4 ounces filling on top of each large muffin cup filled 2/3 full of a basic muffin batter. Swirl filling through batter with knife. Bake muffins as usual.

PINEAPPLE UPSIDE-DOWN GINGER MUFFINS
(See picture, p. 134)

Yield: 8 dozen 3-inch muffins

Ingredients

PINEAPPLE, CRUSHED, well drained	2 quarts
BUTTER or MARGARINE	1 pound
SUGAR, GRANULATED	1 pound
SUGAR, BROWN	1 pound
CORN SYRUP, LIGHT	1 pound
MARASCHINO CHERRIES, halved	96 halves
MUFFIN MIX (PLAIN, BASIC)	5 pounds
PINEAPPLE SYRUP (from canned crushed pineapple)	1-1/2 cups
SOUR CREAM	1 pound (1 quart)
GINGER, POWDERED	2 tablespoons

Procedure

1. Combine pineapple, butter, sugars, and corn syrup. Heat and stir until butter melts and mixture is blended.
2. Grease 8 dozen 3-inch muffin pans. Place a cherry half in bottom of each muffin cup.
3. Place a No. 40 scoop of pineapple mixture over the cherry in each muffin cup.
4. Place muffin mix in mixer bowl. Add pineapple syrup, sour cream and ginger. Mix at low speed 1 minute or until mixture is blended.
5. Portion batter over top of pineapple mixture, using No. 40 scoop.
6. Bake in oven at 425°F. for 20 to 25 minutes or until done. Immediately invert pans; tap bottom of each muffin. Carefully lift up hot pan. Allow muffins to cool.

GINGERBREAD MUFFINS

Yield: 60 2-1/2 inch muffins

Ingredients

FLOUR, ALL-PURPOSE	2 pounds
SODA	2-1/2 teaspoons
CINNAMON	2 teaspoons
CLOVES, GROUND	1 teaspoon
ALLSPICE	1 tablespoon
GINGER	1 tablespoon
SHORTENING	8-1/2 ounces
SUGAR	9 ounces
SALT	3-1/2 teaspoons
EGGS, WHOLE	8 ounces (1 cup)
BUTTERMILK	3 cups
MOLASSES	1-1/2 pounds (2 cups)

Procedure

1. Sift flour, soda and spices together.
2. Cream shortening, sugar and salt thoroughly, scraping down sides of bowl and beater 2 to 3 times.
3. Gradually add eggs; continue beating until light and fluffy.
4. Mix buttermilk and molasses together.
5. Add sifted dry ingredients to creamed mixture; then add buttermilk and molasses mixture. Blend at low speed just long enough for flour to become moistened.
6. Scrape down sides of bowl and beater. Turn mixer to second speed; beat a few seconds longer. Remove bowl from mixer. Finish mixing with a few strokes by hand.
7. Fill well-greased muffin pans, using No. 30 scoop. Bake in oven at 375°F. for 20 to 25 minutes or until done.

GRAHAM MUFFINS

Yield: 18 to 20 muffins

Ingredients

FLOUR, ALL-PURPOSE	12 ounces
SALT	2 teaspoons
BAKING POWDER	2 tablespoons + 2 teaspoons
CINNAMON, GROUND	2 teaspoons
GRAHAM CRACKER CRUMBS	1 quart
SUGAR, LIGHT BROWN	1/2 pound
EGGS, beaten	4
MILK	2 cups
BUTTER or MARGARINE, melted	1-1/3 cups

Procedure

1. Combine flour, salt, baking powder and cinnamon; sift.
2. Add crumbs and sugar; mix well.
3. Add eggs, milk and butter; stir quickly until just mixed but still lumpy.
4. Fill greased muffin cups 2/3 full. Bake in oven at 400°F. for 25 to 30 minutes.

MINCEMEAT MUFFINS

Yield: 40 muffins

Ingredients

BISCUIT MIX	2-1/2 pounds
MINCEMEAT	2-1/2 cups
EGGS	5
SUGAR	1/4 cup
WATER	2 cups

Procedure

1. Combine ingredients. Beat at medium speed 1 minute.
2. Fill heavily greased muffin pans 2/3 full.
3. Bake in oven at 400°F. for 20 minutes or until done.

PEANUT BUTTER APPLE MUFFINS

Yield: 8 dozen 2-inch muffins

Ingredients

SUGAR	1-1/2 pounds
CINNAMON, GROUND	1/4 ounce
SHORTENING	6 ounces
PEANUT BUTTER	6 ounces
EGGS	10 ounces
FLOUR, CAKE	3 pounds, 6 ounces
BAKING POWDER	3-1/4 ounces
SALT	1 ounce
MILK	1-1/2 quarts
APPLES, chopped	2 pounds

Procedure

1. Mix sugar and cinnamon. Reserve 6 ounces (or 1/4 the amount) for topping.

2. Cream shortening and peanut butter with remaining cinnamon sugar until light and fluffy.

3. Add eggs, beat well.

4. Sift flour, baking powder and salt together.

5. Add flour mixture and milk all at once to creamed mixture; mix until just blended.

6. Fold in apples.

7. Put batter into greased muffin pans. Sprinkle top with reserved cinnamon sugar.

8. Bake in oven at 425°F. for 20 to 25 minutes, until done.

134   BREAKFAST AND BRUNCH DISHES

Pineapple Upside-Down Ginger Muffins (See recipe, p. 130)

Dole Pineapple

CHERRY CORN MUFFINS

Yield: 8 dozen

Ingredients

CORN MEAL	2 pounds
FLOUR, ALL-PURPOSE	5 pounds
SUGAR	1-1/2 pounds
BAKING POWDER	5 ounces
SALT	5 teaspoons
RED SOUR CHERRIES (WATER PACK)	1 No. 10 can
SUGAR	1/2 cup
EGGS, slightly beaten	12
MILK	2 quarts
BUTTER, melted	1 pound

Procedure

1. Combine corn meal, flour, first amount of sugar, baking powder and salt in mixer bowl. Mix at low speed about 5 minutes.
2. Drain cherries; sprinkle with remaining sugar. Add to flour mixture.
3. Combine eggs, milk and butter. Add, all at once, to flour mixture; mix only until dampened.
4. Portion with a No. 16 scoop into greased muffin cups.
5. Bake in oven at 400°F. for 25 minutes or until done.

OLD-FASHIONED FILBERT NUT MUFFINS

Yield: 36 pounds batter (290 muffins)

Ingredients	
SUGAR	5 pounds
SHORTENING	2-1/4 pounds
SODA	3-3/4 ounces
SALT	3-3/4 ounces
EGGS	2-1/2 pounds
MOLASSES (LIGHT)	5-1/2 pounds
WATER	10-1/2 ounces
FLOUR, BREAD	10 pounds
BAKING POWDER	7-1/4 ounces
FLOUR, WHOLE WHEAT	4 pounds, 6-1/2 ounces
FILBERTS, chopped	5 pounds
ORANGE RIND, grated	4-1/2 ounces

Procedure

1. Combine sugar, shortening, soda, salt and eggs; cream together thoroughly.
2. Blend in molasses and water.
3. Sift flour and baking powder; add to molasses mixture.
4. Add whole wheat flour, chopped filberts and grated orange rind; blend thoroughly.
5. Fill greased or paper-lined muffin cups allowing 2 ounces per muffin. If desired, sprinkle tops with crushed or sliced filberts or with a combination of two parts nuts and one part sugar.
6. Bake in oven at 380°F. for 23 to 28 minutes or until done. Dust tops with confectioners' sugar, if desired.

CARAWAY CHEESE MUFFINS ⟶

Yield: 6 dozen muffins

Ingredients

FLOUR	3 pounds (3 quarts, sifted)
BAKING POWDER	2-1/2 ounces (6-1/2 tablespoons)
SALT	4 teaspoons
SUGAR	1 cup
SHORTENING	14 ounces (2 cups)
CHEESE, AMERICAN, SHARP, grated	12 ounces
CARAWAY SEEDS	2 tablespoons
EGGS, beaten	6 (1-1/4 cups)
MILK	1-1/4 quarts

PEANUT BUTTER BRAN MUFFINS

Yield: 4 dozen 2-ounce muffins

Ingredients

FLOUR, ALL-PURPOSE	1 pound
BAKING POWDER	1/4 cup
SALT	2 teaspoons
SUGAR	7 ounces (1 cup)
EGGS, unbeaten	6 (10 ounces)
PEANUT BUTTER	1 pound (1-1/2 cups)
MILK	1 quart
BRAN FLAKES	2 quarts (11 ounces)

Procedure

1. Sift flour, baking powder, salt and sugar together.
2. Combine eggs and peanut butter; add milk gradually, blending well.
3. Add egg mixture to flour mixture; mix only enough to dampen flour. Fold in cereal.
4. Turn into greased muffin pans, using a No. 24 scoop or filling pans 2/3 full.
5. Bake in oven at 400°F. for 20 minutes or until done.

Procedure
1. Sift flour, baking powder, salt and sugar together.
2. Cut in shortening until finely divided and mixture resembles coarse meal. (Use pastry blender by hand or, on mixer, use pastry cutter or paddle at low speed.)
3. Add cheese and caraway; mix until evenly distributed.
4. Combine eggs and milk. Add to flour mixture, mixing only enough to dampen dry ingredients.
5. Turn batter into greased muffin pans, using a level No. 24 scoop. Or, fill pans 2/3 full. Bake in oven at 400°F. for 20 to 25 minutes.

BRANANA MUFFINS

Yield: 36 medium-size muffins

Ingredients

WHOLE BRAN CEREAL	3 cups
MILK	3/4 cup
BANANAS, RIPE, mashed	3 cups
EGGS	3
SHORTENING, soft	3/4 cup
FLOUR, ALL-PURPOSE	12 ounces (3 cups, sifted)
BAKING POWDER	2-1/2 tablespoons
SALT	1-1/2 teaspoons
SUGAR	3/4 cup

Procedure
1. Combine bran cereal, milk and mashed bananas. Add eggs and shortening; beat well.
2. Sift together flour, baking powder, salt and sugar. Add to banana mixture; mix only until ingredients are combined.
3. Fill greased muffin pans 2/3 full. Bake in oven at 400°F. for about 30 minutes.

Date-Starred Muffins

Pillsbury Co.

BRAN MUFFINS

Yield: 4 dozen

Ingredients

ENRICHED WHOLE BRAN	1 pound
MILK	1-3/4 quarts
SHORTENING	8 ounces
SUGAR	1 pound
EGGS	8
FLOUR	2 pounds
BAKING POWDER	3 ounces (1/2 cup)
SALT	1 tablespoon

Procedure
1. Soak bran in milk while preparing creamed mixture.
2. Cream shortening and sugar until light and fluffy. Beat in eggs until smooth.
3. Beat in bran mixture.
4. Sift together flour, baking powder and salt; add to bran mixture. Mix only enough to dampen flour thoroughly.
5. Fill well-greased large muffin pans 2/3 full (about 1/3 cup batter per muffin).
6. Bake in oven at 400°F. for about 25 minutes.

WHOLE BRAN MUFFINS

Yield: 2 dozen 2-1/2 inch muffins

Ingredients

WHOLE BRAN BASIC MIX	1 pound, 10 ounces
EGGS	2
MILK	1-3/4 cups

Procedure

1. Place mix in mixing bowl.
2. Add eggs to milk; beat well. Add liquid to mix, stir only until combined. Fill well-greased muffin pans about 2/3 full using a No. 20 scoop.
3. Bake in oven at 400°F. for about 25 minutes or until nicely browned. Serve hot.

Note

For Pan Bread, pour batter in a greased 16-inch by 10-inch by 2-inch pan. Bake in oven at 400°F. for about 35 minutes or until nicely browned. Cut in squares, serve hot.

Variations

Date, Fig or Raisin: Add 1 cup of chopped dates, figs or raisins to 1 pound 10 ounces Whole Bran Mix before adding liquid.

Nut: Add 1 cup chopped nuts to 1 pound 10 ounces Whole Bran Mix before adding liquid.

Jam-Bran: Press 1 teaspoon jam into top of each muffin before baking.

Upside-down: Place 1/2 teaspoon melted butter, 1 teaspoon brown sugar and 1 prune or apricot (cut side down) in bottom of each greased muffin cup before filling with batter.

BASIC WHOLE BRAN MUFFIN MIX ⟶

Yield: Mix for 12 dozen muffins

Ingredients

FLOUR	4 pounds
BAKING POWDER	4 ounces (2/3 cup)
SALT	1-1/4 ounces (2-1/2 tablespoons)
SUGAR	1 pound, 12 ounces (1 quart)
SHORTENING, HYDROGENATED (at room temperature)	2 pounds
WHOLE BRAN CEREAL	2 pounds (2 16-ounce packages)

JELLY TOPPED ALMOND MUFFINS

Yield: 6 dozen

Ingredients

FLOUR	3 pounds
BAKING POWDER	6 tablespoons (2-1/4 ounces)
SUGAR	1 cup
SALT	1-1/2 tablespoons
SHORTENING	1 pound, 2 ounces
EGGS, well beaten	6 (10 ounces)
MILK	1-1/4 quarts
JELLY	1-1/2 cups
WHOLE UNBLANCHED ALMONDS	10 ounces

Procedure

1. Sift flour, baking powder, sugar and salt together.
2. Cut in shortening until mixture resembles coarse meal.
3. Combine eggs and milk. Add to flour mixture, mixing only enough to blend.
4. Turn into greased muffin pans, using a well-rounded No. 30 scoop or filling pans 2/3 full.
5. Press 1 teaspoon jelly into top of each muffin. Arrange three whole unblanched almonds around top of each muffin, petal fashion.
6. Bake in oven at 400°F. for 25 to 30 minutes.

Procedure

1. Sift flour, baking powder, salt and sugar into large mixer bowl.
2. Add shortening. Mix, using paddle at low speed, until well blended. Add cereal; stir until distributed.
3. Store in tightly covered containers until ready to use.

Note

Refer to p. 139 for baking procedure.

PUMPKIN MUFFINS

Yield: 5 dozen

Ingredients

FLOUR, sifted	2 quarts (2 pounds)
BAKING POWDER	1/4 cup
SALT	4 teaspoons
SUGAR, GRANULATED	3 cups
CINNAMON	1 tablespoon
NUTMEG	1 tablespoon
MARGARINE	12 ounces
RAISINS, SEEDLESS	3 cups
EGGS, beaten	6
PUMPKIN, CANNED	3 cups
MILK	3 cups
SUGAR, for sprinkling on tops	1/3 to 1/2 cup

Procedure

1. Sift dry ingredients together; cut in margarine; add raisins.
2. Combine beaten eggs, pumpkin and milk; add to dry mixture. Mix lightly, only to combine.
3. Fill greased muffin pans 2/3 full. Sprinkle sugar on each muffin.
4. Bake in oven at 450°F. for 18 to 20 minutes.
5. Serve hot.

PECAN WHOLE WHEAT MUFFINS

Yield: 12 dozen

Ingredients

SUGAR	1-3/4 pounds
SHORTENING	2 pounds
EGG YOLKS	1 pound
FLOUR, ALL-PURPOSE	5 pounds
BAKING POWDER	8 ounces
SALT	3 tablespoons
FLOUR, WHOLE WHEAT	3 pounds
PECANS, chopped	1 pound
MILK	3-1/4 quarts
PECAN HALVES	as needed

Procedure

1. Cream sugar and shortening until light and fluffy.
2. Add egg yolks; mix well.
3. Combine all-purpose flour, baking powder and salt; sift. Add whole wheat flour and chopped pecans; mix well.
4. Add dry ingredients and milk to egg mixture all at one time. Mix only until well blended.
5. Dip with No. 20 scoop into well-greased muffin pans (approximately 2 ounces each). Top each with a pecan half.
6. Bake in oven at 375°F. for 20 to 25 minutes or until done.

YAM NUT MUFFINS

Yield: 10 dozen

Ingredients	
FLOUR, BREAD	3 pounds, 6 ounces
FLOUR, CAKE	1-1/4 pounds
SALT	1-2/3 ounces
BAKING POWDER	5 ounces
SUGAR, BROWN	1/2 pound
WALNUTS, coarsely chopped	1-1/2 pounds
EGGS, beaten	2 pounds
MILK	3-3/4 pounds
YAMS, cooked, mashed	6 pounds
BUTTER or MARGARINE, melted	1-1/4 pounds
CINNAMON, GROUND	as needed
SUGAR, GRANULATED	as needed

Procedure

1. Sift flours, salt and baking powder together. Add brown sugar and nuts; mix well.

2. Combine eggs, milk, yams and butter; mix well.

3. Add yam mixture to dry ingredients all at once; mix only until combined.

4. Fill greased 2-inch muffin pans 2/3 full. Sprinkle lightly with mixture of cinnamon and granulated sugar.

5. Bake in oven at 425°F. for about 25 minutes or until done.

PECAN GEMS

Yield: 5 dozen

Ingredients	
SUGAR, GRANULATED	1 pound
SUGAR, LIGHT BROWN	1 pound
BUTTER or MARGARINE	12 ounces
HONEY	4 ounces
CORN SYRUP	4 ounces
FLOUR, CAKE	1/2 ounce
BASIC MUFFIN MIX	5 pounds
PECANS	as needed

CHERRY MUFFINS

Yield: 5 dozen muffins

Ingredients	
SOUR RED CHERRIES, drained	1-1/4 quarts
SUGAR	1-1/4 cups
FLOUR, sifted	2-1/2 pounds (2-1/2 quarts)
SALT	1-1/2 tablespoons
SODA	1-1/2 tablespoons
SUGAR	1-1/4 cups
EGGS, slightly beaten	5
BUTTERMILK	1-1/4 quarts
BUTTER, melted	1-1/4 cups

Procedure

1. Combine cherries and first amount of sugar; let stand while mixing muffins.

2. Sift flour, salt, soda and second amount of sugar.

3. Combine eggs, buttermilk and melted butter. Add to dry ingredients; mix only until moistened but not smooth. Add cherries; mix lightly.

4. Fill greased muffin pans 2/3 full. Bake in oven at 400°F. for 25 minutes or until done.

Procedure

1. Combine sugars, butter, honey, corn syrup and cake flour; blend to a smooth consistency. Do not cream light. Set aside.

2. Prepare basic muffin mix according to package directions.

3. Place a dot of sugar mixture in bottom of each cup of well-greased gem or muffin pans. Sprinkle 3 to 5 whole (or chopped) pecans over mixture.

4. Fill cups 1/2 to 2/3 full with batter. Bake in oven at 400°F. for 15 to 20 minutes or until centers are set.

5. Invert pans onto sheet pan as soon as removed from oven. Allow pans to remain a few seconds to allow the caramel syrup to flow over the gems. Remove hot pans.

PRUNE MUFFINS

Yield: 6 dozen

Ingredients	
PITTED PRUNES*	1-1/2 pounds
SHORTENING	12 ounces
SUGAR, BROWN	1-1/4 pounds
EGGS	6 (10 ounces)
FLOUR, ALL-PURPOSE	3 pounds
BAKING POWDER	1/4 cup
SALT	2 tablespoons
MILK	4-1/2 cups

Procedure

1. Chop prunes coarsely. (For ease in chopping, add 1 tablespoon salad oil per pound of prunes.)

2. Cream shortening and sugar until light.

3. Beat in eggs. Add prunes.

4. Sift flour, baking powder and salt together. Add to prune mixture alternately with milk.

5. Portion batter into greased or paper-lined 2-1/2-inch muffin pans, using No. 16 scoop.

6. Bake in oven at 400°F. for 18 to 20 minutes, or until done.

*Pitted prunes are available in 12-ounce, 25-pound and 30-pound packages. Do not pre-cook for use in this recipe.

BRAN MUFFINS WITH CRUNCHY TOPPING

Yield: 24 muffins

Ingredients

MUFFIN BATTER

WHOLE BRAN CEREAL	2-1/2 cups
MILK	2 cups
MOLASSES	1/4 cup
FLOUR, ALL-PURPOSE	8 ounces
SALT	1 teaspoon
BAKING POWDER	1 tablespoon
SODA	1/2 teaspoon
SUGAR, DARK BROWN	3 ounces (1/2 cup, packed)
EGGS, beaten	2
BUTTER or MARGARINE, melted	1/4 cup

TOPPING

WHOLE BRAN CEREAL	3/4 cup
SUGAR, DARK BROWN	1/3 cup (packed)
PECANS, coarsely chopped	1/3 cup
BUTTER or MARGARINE, melted	1/3 cup

Procedure

1. Combine bran cereal, milk and molasses; let stand 5 minutes.
2. Sift flour, salt, baking powder and soda. Add sugar; mix well.
3. Add beaten eggs, melted butter and bran mixture; mix only until moistened.
4. Fill well-greased muffin cups 2/3 full.
5. Combine ingredients for topping; sprinkle over muffins. Bake in oven at 400°F. for 30 to 35 minutes.

CRANBERRY-ORANGE MUFFINS

Yield: 6 dozen

Ingredients

CRANBERRIES, FRESH or FROZEN, chopped	1-1/2 quarts
SUGAR	3 cups
FLOUR, sifted	3 quarts
BAKING POWDER	6 tablespoons
SUGAR	3/4 cup
SALT	2 tablespoons
EGGS, beaten	6
MILK	1-1/2 quarts
SHORTENING, melted	3/4 cup
ORANGE RIND, grated	6 tablespoons

Procedure

1. Combine cranberries and first amount of sugar. Allow to stand while preparing remaining ingredients.

2. Sift flour, baking powder, remaining sugar and salt together.

3. Combine eggs, milk, shortening and orange rind. Add, all at once, to dry ingredients; mix just until flour is moistened. Add cranberries with last few mixing strokes.

4. Fill greased muffin pans, filling cups 2/3 full. Bake in oven at 400°F. for 25 minutes or until done.

Colorful Corn Sticks and Corn Muffins in Roll Basket

Pillsbury Co.

Corn Breads

CORN STICKS

Yield: 40 sticks

Ingredients

CORN MEAL, WHITE	1 quart
BAKING POWDER	4 teaspoons
SODA	2 teaspoons
SALT	1 tablespoon
BUTTERMILK	1 quart
EGGS, unbeaten	4
SHORTENING, melted	2/3 cup

Procedure

1. Combine corn meal, baking powder, soda and salt.
2. Add buttermilk, eggs and shortening; mix well.
3. Turn batter into hot greased iron corn stick pans. Bake in oven at 450°F. for 20 minutes or until done.

BREAKFAST AND BRUNCH DISHES

SPOONBREAD ⟶

Yield: 25 portions

Ingredients
CORN MEAL	8 ounces (1-1/2 cups)
TAPIOCA, QUICK-COOKING	2 tablespoons
SALT	2 teaspoons
MILK	2 quarts
BUTTER or MARGARINE	4 ounces
EGG YOLKS	8 (2/3 cup)
EGG WHITES	8 (1 cup)

PINEAPPLE CORN BREAD

Yield: 100 portions

Ingredients
FLOUR, ALL-PURPOSE	3 pounds
CORN MEAL	4-3/4 pounds
NONFAT DRY MILK	1 pound
SUGAR	1-1/2 pounds
BAKING POWDER	8 ounces (1-1/3 cup)
SALT	3 ounces (6 tablespoons)
EGGS	16 (3-1/3 cups)
PINEAPPLE, CRUSHED, undrained	1 No. 10 can
SHORTENING, melted	1 pound, 2 ounces
WATER	1-1/2 quarts

Procedure

1. Blend flour, corn meal, dry milk, sugar, baking powder and salt in mixer on low speed 5 minutes.
2. Add eggs, undrained crushed pineapple, shortening and water. Beat at low speed just until moistened.
3. Pour into 4 well-greased 12-inch by 20-inch by 2-inch baking pans allowing about 5-1/2 pounds per pan.
4. Bake in oven at 425°F. for about 25 minutes or until done.

Procedure

1. Combine corn meal, tapioca, salt and milk in top of double boiler or in heavy saucepan. Cook, stirring constantly, until consistency of mush.
2. Stir in butter. Remove from heat. Cool slightly.
3. Beat egg yolks well; blend into corn meal mixture.
4. Beat egg whites until stiff; fold into batter.
5. Turn into greased 12-inch by 20-inch by 2-inch baking pan. Bake in oven at 375°F. for 45 minutes or until done.

CORN-HOMINY STICKS

Yield: 5 dozen

Ingredients

FLOUR, ALL-PURPOSE, sifted	3 cups (12 ounces)
CORN MEAL	1 quart
BAKING POWDER	1/4 cup
SALT	1 tablespoon
HOMINY, hot boiled	2 cups
MARGARINE, melted	1/2 pound
MILK	1 quart
EGGS, beaten	4

Procedure

1. Sift flour, corn meal, baking powder and salt. Add the hot hominy.
2. Make a well in center of mixture; add melted margarine, milk and beaten egg. Mix until blended.
3. Pour into very well-greased bread stick pans. Bake in oven at 350°F. for 25 minutes, or until nicely browned.

SOUTHERN CORN BREAD

Yield: 1 18-inch by 26-inch pan or 7 dozen corn sticks

Ingredients
CORN MEAL, WHITE	2 quarts
BAKING POWDER	3 tablespoons
SODA	4 teaspoons
SALT	2 tablespoons
BUTTERMILK	2 quarts
EGGS, unbeaten	8
SHORTENING, melted	1-1/3 cups

Procedure
1. Combine corn meal, baking powder, soda and salt. Mix thoroughly.
2. Add buttermilk, eggs and shortening. Mix well.
3. Turn into a well-greased 18-inch by 26-inch by 1-inch pan; bake in oven at 425°F. for 35 to 40 minutes or until done.

Corn Sticks: turn the batter into hot well-greased iron corn stick pans. Bake in oven at 450°F. for 20 minutes.

SESAME CHEESE CORN BREAD

Yield: 1 12-inch by 18-inch pan

Ingredients
EGGS	5
WATER	1-1/2 pounds
CORN BREAD MIX	2-1/2 pounds
CHEESE, CHEDDAR, grated	10 ounces
SALT	1-1/2 teaspoons
SESAME SEEDS	1/2 cup

Procedure
1. Blend eggs and water in bowl. Add corn bread mix, cheese and salt. Blend until smooth. Do not overmix.
2. Pour into greased 12-inch by 18-inch baking pan. Sprinkle batter with sesame seeds.
3. Bake in oven at 450°F. for 15 minutes or until done.

SWEET POTATO PONE

Yield: 24 portions

Ingredients

SWEET POTATOES, raw, grated	2 quarts
SUGAR	3 cups
NUTMEG	1 tablespoon
SALT	1 tablespoon
PECANS, chopped	2 cups
EGGS, well beaten	8
MILK	1 quart
BUTTER	1/4 pound

Procedure

1. Combine sweet potatoes, sugar, nutmeg, salt and pecans; mix.
2. Combine eggs and milk. Add to sweet potato mixture.
3. Pour into a well-buttered 12-inch by 20-inch by 2-inch baking pan. Dot with butter.
4. Bake in oven at 350°F. for 45 minutes to 1 hour or until set.

Coffee Cakes

Vary with Crunchy Toppings, Surprise Bits in Batter

Pillsbury Food Service

HONEY NUT COFFEE CAKE

Yield: 40 portions

Ingredients	
SHORTENING	1 pound, 4 ounces
SUGAR, LIGHT BROWN	2 pounds, 9 ounces
FLOUR	2 pounds, 8 ounces
SALT	1-3/4 teaspoons
CINNAMON	2 teaspoons
NUTMEG	2 teaspoons
WALNUTS, coarsely chopped	1 pound
SODA	1/2 ounce (4 teaspoons)
EGGS, slightly beaten	5
HONEY	3/4 cup
BUTTERMILK	3-1/2 cups

Procedure

1. Cream shortening and sugar until very light and smooth.

2. Combine flour, salt and spices; mix well. Add to shortening mixture; mix on low speed until blended and mixture is lumpy. Add nuts; mix until just blended.

3. Remove 11 ounces of the mixture. Set aside for topping.

4. Mix soda into remaining mixture just enough to blend well. Mixture will be fine and crumbly at this stage.

5. Combine eggs, honey and buttermilk. Mix into dry ingredients by hand or on low speed of mixer just until flour is moistened.

6. Spread in greased and floured 18-inch by 26-inch sheet pan. Sprinkle with topping.

7. Bake in oven at 375°F. until lightly browned and done, about 35 minutes. Cut cake 5 x 8 for 40 portions.

GRAHAM-NUT COFFEECAKE

Yield: 4 cakes—64 1-3/4 inch slices

Ingredients

ACTIVE DRY YEAST	2 ounces
WATER, warm	2 cups
MILK, scalded	1 quart
SUGAR	2 cups
SALT	2-1/2 tablespoons
BUTTER or MARGARINE, cut into pieces	1 pound
EGGS, beaten	8
FLOUR, ALL-PURPOSE	4 pounds
GRAHAM CRACKER CRUMBS	2 pounds
BUTTER or MARGARINE	1 pound
WALNUTS or PECANS, chopped	2 pounds
CINNAMON, GROUND	4 teaspoons
GRAHAM CRACKER CRUMBS	1 pound
SUGAR	1 cup
DATES, chopped	2 pounds

Procedure

1. Sprinkle yeast onto water. Stir to dissolve.
2. Combine milk, first amount of sugar, salt and first amount of butter. Cool to lukewarm; stir in eggs and yeast.
3. Stir in half the flour; then remaining flour and first amount of graham cracker crumbs. Beat until smooth and elastic.
4. Cover; let rise in a warm place (80° to 85°F.) until double in bulk.
5. Melt remaining butter.
6. Combine nuts, cinnamon, remaining cracker crumbs and remaining sugar.
7. Punch down risen dough; stir in chopped dates.
8. Using 2 teaspoons, break off pieces of dough. Turn pieces in melted butter, then in nut mixture. Place in greased 10-inch tube pans, dividing equally among 4 pans.
9. Let rise in a warm place until double in bulk.
10. Bake in oven at 350°F. for 45 to 50 minutes, or until done. Cool in pan 10 minutes. Remove; cool on rack.

ORANGE COFFEE CAKE

Yield: 1 16-inch by 10-inch pan (20 portions)

Ingredients

FLOUR, ALL-PURPOSE	10 ounces
BAKING POWDER	4 teaspoons
SALT	1 teaspoon
SHORTENING, soft	1/2 cup
SUGAR, GRANULATED	1 cup
EGGS	2
ORANGE RIND, grated	4 teaspoons
ALMOND FLAVORING	1/4 teaspoon
WHOLE BRAN CEREAL	1 cup
ORANGE JUICE	1/2 cup
MILK	1/2 cup
FLOUR, sifted	2/3 cup
SUGAR, LIGHT BROWN	6 ounces
ORANGE RIND, grated	2 tablespoons
BUTTER or MARGARINE, soft	2 ounces

Procedure

1. Combine first amount of flour, baking powder and salt; sift.
2. Blend shortening and granulated sugar, beating 3 minutes on 2nd speed of mixer.
3. Add eggs, first amount of orange rind and almond flavoring; beat at 2nd speed 1 minute. Add bran, orange juice and milk; mix until combined.
4. Add sifted ingredients; mix at 1st speed only until blended.
5. Spread batter in greased 16-inch by 10-inch by 2-inch pan.
6. Combine remaining flour, brown sugar and orange rind. Add butter; cut in until mixture resembles coarse corn meal.
7. Sprinkle evenly over batter in pan; press lightly.
8. Bake in oven at 375°F. for about 20 minutes. Serve warm.

RAISIN COFFEE CAKE

Yield: 24 portions

Ingredients

FLOUR, ALL-PURPOSE	1-1/4 pounds
BAKING POWDER	2 tablespoons
SALT	2-1/2 teaspoons
SUGAR	1 cup
SHORTENING	1 cup
RAISINS	2/3 cup
ORANGE RIND, grated	1-1/2 teaspoons
EGGS, well beaten	3
MILK	2-1/2 cups
SUGAR, BROWN	1/3 cup (packed)
CINNAMON	1/2 teaspoon
NUTMEG	1/4 teaspoon

Procedure

1. Sift flour, baking powder, salt and sugar together.
2. Cut in shortening until mixture looks like coarse meal. Add raisins and orange rind.
3. Combine eggs and milk; add to flour mixture. Mix only until all flour is dampened.
4. Turn into 3 greased 9-inch layer cake pans.
5. Mix brown sugar, cinnamon and nutmeg. Sprinkle over batter.
6. Bake in oven at 425°F. for 15 to 20 minutes or until done. Cut in wedges. Serve warm.

HONEY CRISP COFFEE CAKE

Yield: 100 portions, 5 16-inch by 10-inch by 2-inch pans

Ingredients
FLOUR	3-3/4 pounds
BAKING POWDER	1/3 cup plus 1 tablespoon
SALT	3 tablespoons
SHORTENING	1 pound
SUGAR	1-1/2 pounds
EGGS	10 (2 cups)
MILK	1-3/4 quarts
CORN FLAKES, SUGAR-COATED	10 ounces
BUTTER or MARGARINE, soft	1-2/3 cups
HONEY	2-1/2 cups
COCONUT, SHREDDED	2-1/2 cups
PINEAPPLE, CRUSHED, drained	1-1/4 quarts

Procedure

1. Sift flour with baking powder and salt.
2. Cream shortening and sugar. Add eggs; beat well.
3. Add sifted dry ingredients alternately with milk. Do not overmix. Spread batter in five greased 16-inch by 10-inch by 2-inch pans.
4. Crush cereal slightly.
5. Blend butter and honey. Add coconut, pineapple and cereal. Sprinkle evenly over batter.
6. Bake in oven at 400°F. for 35 minutes or until done. Serve warm.

CHERRY RAISIN COFFEE CAKE

Yield: 4 9-inch by 9-inch by 2-inch pans, 48 portions

Ingredients

BISCUIT MIX	2 pounds
SUGAR, GRANULATED	1 cup
SHORTENING, soft	4 ounces
MILK	3 cups
EGGS	4
SUGAR, BROWN	1 cup (6 ounces)
RAISINS	2 cups
CINNAMON	1 teaspoon
CHERRY JAM	2-1/2 cups
CONFECTIONERS' SUGAR	1 pound
VANILLA	2 teaspoons
WATER	3 to 4 tablespoons

Procedure

1. Combine biscuit mix, granulated sugar, shortening, milk and eggs. Mix at low speed for 1 minute.
2. Spread batter into greased 9-inch by 9-inch by 2-inch pans.
3. Combine brown sugar, raisins and cinnamon. Sprinkle over batter in pans.
4. Spoon jam over top.
5. Bake in oven at 400°F. for 20 to 25 minutes, or until done.
6. Combine confectioners' sugar, vanilla and water to make a thin icing.
7. Drizzle over warm coffee cakes.

CRANBERRY NUT SQUARES

Yield: 48 portions, 2 12-inch by 20-inch pans

Ingredients

FLOUR, ALL-PURPOSE	2 pounds
SUGAR	1 quart
BAKING POWDER	2 tablespoons
SODA	2 teaspoons
SALT	1 tablespoon
ALLSPICE, GROUND	1 tablespoon
SHORTENING	1 cup
ORANGE JUICE	3 cups
EGGS, beaten	4
VANILLA	2 teaspoons
CRANBERRIES, FRESH, chopped	1/2 pound
WALNUTS or PECANS, chopped	2 cups

Procedure

1. Combine flour, sugar, baking powder, soda, salt and allspice in bowl; mix well. Cut in shortening until mixture resembles coarse meal.

2. Combine orange juice, eggs and vanilla. Add to dry mixture; mix only until dampened.

3. Fold in cranberries and nuts.

4. Turn batter into two greased 12-inch by 20-inch pans. Bake in oven at 350°F. for 55 to 60 minutes or until done.

HAWAIIAN BREAKFAST COFFEE CAKE

Yield: 30 portions

Ingredients

BISCUIT MIX	1 quart
SUGAR, GRANULATED	1/2 cup
GINGER, GROUND	1 teaspoon
CINNAMON, GROUND	1 teaspoon
LIQUID SHORTENING	1/4 cup
MILK	1-1/2 cups
EGGS	2
PINEAPPLE, CRUSHED, drained	2 cups
SUGAR, BROWN	1 cup
COCONUT	1 cup
WALNUTS, chopped	1/2 cup
GINGER, CANDIED, chopped	2 tablespoons
CINNAMON, GROUND	1/2 teaspoon

Procedure

1. Combine biscuit mix, granulated sugar, ground ginger and first amount of cinnamon; mix.
2. Combine shortening, milk and eggs. Add to dry ingredients; mix just until blended.
3. Turn into oiled 10-inch by 16-inch baking pan.
4. Mix remaining ingredients; spoon over batter.
5. Bake in oven at 400°F. for 25 minutes or until done.

CINNAMON CRUMB COFFEE CAKE

Yield: 20 portions

Ingredients

FLOUR	1 pound
BAKING POWDER	4 teaspoons
SALT	1-1/2 teaspoons
CINNAMON	1 tablespoon
SUGAR	1-1/2 cups
EGGS, slightly beaten	2
MILK	1-1/2 cups
SHORTENING, melted	1 cup
CORN FLAKE CRUMBS	1 cup
BUTTER or MARGARINE, melted	1/4 cup
SUGAR	1/2 cup
CINNAMON	1 teaspoon

Procedure

1. Sift flour with baking powder, salt, first amounts of cinnamon and sugar.

2. Combine eggs and milk; add to flour mixture together with shortening. Mix only until combined. Spread in a greased 16-inch by 10-inch baking pan.

3. Mix corn flake crumbs, butter, remaining sugar and cinnamon. Press lightly into batter.

4. Bake in oven at 375°F. for about 45 minutes or until done.

BREAKFAST COFFEE CAKE ⟶

Yield: 2 pans 18-inch by 26-inch by 1-inch, 100 portions

Ingredients

PRUNES, pitted	2 pounds
MUFFIN MIX (PLAIN, BASIC)	5 pounds
SOUR CREAM	1-1/2 quarts
EGGS, beaten	1 pound
CINNAMON	2 tablespoons
SUGAR	1 pound

CARAMEL DATE COFFEE CAKE

Yield: 1 16-inch by 24-inch sheet pan

Ingredients

BASIC MUFFIN MIX	5 pounds
DATES, washed, ground	1-1/2 pounds
WATER	1 quart (2 pounds)

Procedure

1. Place basic muffin mix in bowl. Add dates and one-half of the total water. Mix on low speed to incorporate.

2. Mix on medium speed 2 minutes. Scrape bowl. Add remaining water on low speed to incorporate. Continue mixing for 2 more minutes on medium speed.

3. Turn batter into 16-inch by 24-inch sheet pan or scale 12 ounces of batter per 8-inch greased and floured round layer pan. Top with Butter Crumb Topping.* Bake in oven at 375° to 400°F. for about 30 minutes.

Note

For Date Orange Coffee Cake, use 12 ounces ground washed dates and 12 ounces finely ground fresh whole oranges (wash before grinding) in place of the 1-1/2 pounds ground washed dates.

*See recipe for Butter Crumb Topping page 221.

Procedure

1. Chop prunes. Set aside.
2. Combine muffin mix, sour cream and eggs in a mixer bowl; beat, using paddle at low speed, until batter is almost, but not quite, smooth.
3. Turn batter into 2 greased 18-inch by 26-inch by 1-inch pans allowing about 4-1/2 pounds in each.
4. Distribute chopped prunes over top of batter, dividing equally between the 2 pans.
5. Mix cinnamon and sugar. Sprinkle half over each pan.
6. Bake in oven at 450°F. for 25 to 30 minutes or until done.
7. Allow to cool 5 minutes. Cut each pan 5 x 10 to yield 50 portions.

APPLE COFFEE CAKE

Yield: 1 18-inch by 26-inch pan

Ingredients

MUFFIN MIX (PLAIN, BASIC)	5 pounds
WATER	2-1/4 pounds
LEMON EXTRACT	1 teaspoon
APPLES, chopped	1-1/4 pounds
SUGAR, GRANULATED	6 ounces
BUTTER or MARGARINE, softened	6 ounces
CORN SYRUP, LIGHT	2 tablespoons
VANILLA	1 teaspoon
YELLOW FOOD COLORING	few drops
FLOUR	12 ounces

Procedure

1. Prepare muffin mix with water following package directions; add lemon extract. Fold in apples.
2. Turn batter into 18-inch by 26-inch sheet pan.
3. Combine sugar, butter, corn syrup, vanilla and yellow coloring; mix together.
4. Add flour; rub in by hand until crumbly.
5. Sprinkle topping over batter. Bake in oven at 375°F. for 30 minutes or until done.

APPLE-ROLLED OATS COFFEE CAKE

Yield: 54 portions (3 9-inch by 14-inch by 2-1/2-inch pans)

Ingredients	
EGGS, beaten	6
MILK	1 quart
SHORTENING, melted	1 cup
ROLLED OATS	1 quart
FLOUR, ALL-PURPOSE, sifted	1 pound, 12 ounces (1-3/4 quarts)
SUGAR, GRANULATED	2-1/2 cups
BAKING POWDER	2 ounces (6 tablespoons, scant)
SALT	2 tablespoons
APPLE SLICES, drained	1 No. 10 can
SUGAR, BROWN	1-1/2 cups
SUGAR, GRANULATED	1-1/2 cups
CINNAMON	1 tablespoon
SUGAR, CONFECTIONERS', sifted	1 pound
LEMON JUICE	1/2 cup

Procedure

1. Mix beaten eggs, milk and melted shortening. Add rolled oats.
2. Sift flour, first amount of granulated sugar, baking powder and salt into mixer bowl. Add egg mixture; mix with paddle at low speed only until flour is moistened.
3. Turn batter into 3 well-greased 9-inch by 14-inch by 2-1/2-inch pans allowing 2-1/2 pounds batter per pan.
4. Arrange 1 quart drained apple slices on top of batter in each pan.
5. Mix brown sugar, remaining granulated sugar and cinnamon. Sprinkle 1 cup sugar-cinnamon mixture over each pan.
6. Bake in oven at 375°F. for about 30 minutes or until done.
7. Combine confectioners' sugar and lemon juice. Drizzle over coffee cake. Serve warm, cut in squares.

Rose-Colored Peach Coffee Cake

Pillsbury Co.

MINCEMEAT COFFEE CAKE

Yield: 48 portions

Ingredients	
FLOUR, ALL-PURPOSE	2-3/4 pounds
BAKING POWDER	1/4 cup
SUGAR	2 pounds, 3 ounces
SALT	2 teaspoons
BUTTER or MARGARINE	1 pound
EGGS, slightly beaten	6
MINCEMEAT, PREPARED	1-1/2 pounds (2-1/4 cups)
MILK	1-1/2 cups
SUGAR	1/2 cup
CINNAMON	2 teaspoons

Procedure
1. Sift flour, baking powder, sugar and salt.
2. Cut in butter until the size of coarse corn meal.
3. Combine eggs, mincemeat and milk. Add to flour mixture; mix just enough to combine.
4. Turn into 2 greased 12-inch by 18-inch by 2-inch baking pans.
5. Mix sugar and cinnamon; sprinkle over top of batter. Bake in oven at 375°F. for 45 minutes or until cake is done.

DUTCH APPLE COFFEE CAKE

Yield: 8-1/2 pounds batter, 11 8-inch cakes

Ingredients
BASIC MUFFIN MIX	5 pounds
APPLES, CANNED	1-1/2 pounds
LEMON EXTRACT	1 tablespoon
WATER, at 72°F.	1 quart
BUTTER CRUMB TOPPING*	1 pound

Procedure

1. Place basic muffin mix and apples into mixer bowl. Add half of the water and the lemon extract; mix 2 minutes, using paddle at medium speed. Reduce to low speed; add remaining water; scrape bowl. Mix 2 more minutes on medium speed.

2. Scale 12 ounces of batter per 8-inch round greased and floured layer pan or 8-1/2 pounds batter into a greased 16-inch by 24-inch sheet pan.

3. Top with butter crumb topping. Bake in oven at 375° to 400°F. for about 30 minutes. Dust top with confectioners' sugar or dribble with plain sugar icing over top while slightly warm.

Note

12 ounces of currants or midget raisins, washed and drained, may be added at the end of the mixing, if desired.

*See recipe for Butter Crumb Topping page 221.

Iced and Spiced Loaf Bread

Pillsbury Co.

Quick Loaf Breads

QUICK OR TEA breads baked in the shape of a loaf are a spin-off from the muffin group. They are often made with cereals or a novelty flour and they usually contain nuts and/or fruits. These breads are the outstanding exception to the quick bread serve-it-hot rule. (Boston Brown Bread, however, is the exception to the exception. It is traditionally made in a cylindrical shape, is steamed rather than baked, and is at its delicious best when warm.)

Most tea breads slice more easily and actually taste better if they are made ahead, wrapped in foil and stored overnight. Many of them freeze well. They will keep for weeks, stored in the freezer.

For loaves with even, well-rounded contours, make a depression in the center top of the batter with the tip of a spoon, running it an inch or so short of each end; then branch off, carrying the depression toward the corners of the pan. It's characteristic of many of these loaves to come from the oven with a fairly deep crack in the top.

Tea breads make a welcome addition to the brunch menu. Spread with butter or whipped cream cheese as sandwiches, *they go well with coffee or other beverages and make a novel change for the coffee break.*

NUT BREAD

Yield: 50 portions (6 small loaves)

Ingredients	
SHORTENING	1 cup
SUGAR, BROWN	3 cups
EGGS	4
FLOUR, sifted	2 quarts (2 pounds)
SALT	1-1/2 tablespoons
BAKING POWDER	1/4 cup
SODA	1 tablespoon
BUTTERMILK	1-1/2 quarts
ROLLED OATS, uncooked (quick or old-fashioned)	1 quart
NUT MEATS, chopped	2 cups

Procedure

1. Cream shortening and sugar in mixer about 1 minute at medium speed.

2. Add eggs; continue beating at medium speed about 30 seconds.

3. Sift flour, salt, baking powder and soda. Add sifted dry ingredients and buttermilk to creamed mixture; beat at low speed about 30 seconds. Scrape bottom of bowl once or twice. Do not overbeat.

4. Add rolled oats and nut meats; beat at low speed until distributed, about 15 seconds.

5. Bake in 6 greased paper-lined bread pans (1 pound size) in oven at 350°F. for about 1 hour. Cool; wrap and store one day before slicing.

PRUNE BREAD

Yield: 3 loaves, 10-inch by 4-inch by 4-inch

Ingredients	
BUTTER or MARGARINE	1/3 cup
HONEY	1 cup
SUGAR	1/2 cup
EGGS	8
FLOUR, ALL-PURPOSE	12 ounces (3 cups, sifted)
BAKING POWDER	1-1/2 tablespoons
SALT	1-1/2 teaspoons
SODA	1-1/2 teaspoons
FLOUR, WHOLE WHEAT	9-1/2 ounces (2 cups)
BUTTERMILK	1-1/2 cups
PRUNES, cooked, coarsely chopped	1-1/2 cups
PECANS, chopped	1-1/2 cups
LEMON RIND, grated	1-1/2 teaspoons

Procedure

1. Cream butter, honey and sugar at medium speed for 5 minutes.
2. Add eggs; beat until well blended (3 minutes on mixer).
3. Sift flour, baking powder, salt and soda. Add to whole wheat flour; blend.
4. Add dry ingredients and buttermilk alternately to the creamed mixture; beat until blended. Add prunes, nuts and lemon rind.
5. Turn into three greased loaf pans 10-inch by 4-inch by 4-inch. Bake in oven at 350°F. for 1 hour 10 minutes or until done.

BANANA TEA BREAD OR MUFFINS ⟶

Yield: 24 1-pound loaves or 24 dozen large muffins

Ingredients

BANANAS, mashed	7 pounds, 4 ounces
MARGARINE, softened	2 pounds
SUGAR	5 pounds
EGGS	2-1/2 pounds
WATER	1 pound (about)*
FLOUR, ALL-PURPOSE or BREAD	7-1/2 pounds
BAKING POWDER**	2-1/2 ounces
SODA	2 ounces
PECANS, chopped (optional)	1-1/2 pounds

BUTTERSCOTCH RAISIN BREAD

Yield: 4 loaves, 4-3/4-inch by 8-3/4-inch, about 20 slices each

Ingredients

RAISINS, LIGHT or DARK	2 cups
FLOUR, ALL-PURPOSE	2 quarts
SODA	2 teaspoons
BAKING POWDER	4 teaspoons
SALT	1 tablespoon
EGGS	4
SUGAR, BROWN	1-1/2 pounds
SHORTENING, melted	1/2 cup
BUTTERMILK	1 quart (about)
NUT MEATS, chopped (optional)	1 cup

Procedure

1. Rinse and dry raisins, chop coarsely.

2. Sift flour, soda, baking powder and salt together; add raisins. Beat eggs; add sugar and shortening gradually, beating after each addition.

3. Add flour mixture alternately with buttermilk. Mix just to a smooth batter; avoid over-mixing. Fold in nuts, if desired. Bake in greased loaf pans in oven at 350°F. for 1 hour.

Procedure

1. Mix bananas, margarine, sugar, eggs and water. (*Amount of water variable with flour strength)

2. Sift or thoroughly mix flour, baking powder and soda together. Add dry ingredients and nuts to banana mixture; mix just until all flour is dampened.

3. Fill greased pans half full before batter puffs. Allow 1 pound, 2 ounces batter per 1-pound loaf pan. Bake in oven at 350°F. for 45 minutes or until done. Use No. 24 scoop for muffins. Bake in oven at 375°F. for 20 minutes or until done.

**For muffins, increase baking powder to 5 ounces.

BOSTON BROWN BREAD

Yield: 100 portions

Ingredients

FLOUR, WHOLE WHEAT	2 pounds, 12 ounces (2-1/2 quarts)
CORN MEAL	12 ounces (2-1/4 cups)
BAKING POWDER	1/3 cup
SODA	4 teaspoons
SALT	2 tablespoons
MOLASSES	3-1/2 cups
SHORTENING, melted	1 cup
BUTTERMILK	2-1/4 quarts
RAISINS, SEEDLESS (optional)	1 pound (3 cups)

Procedure

1. Mix dry ingredients. Add molasses and melted shortening; stir well until mixed. Add buttermilk gradually. Add raisins, if desired.

2. Pour batter into well-greased pans; cover loosely. (Type pan is optional. Pans may be deep round pans, such as a 46-ounce can, or regular loaf pans.)

3. Place in steamer at 5 to 6 pounds pressure for 2-1/2 to 3 hours.

SPICED BUTTERSCOTCH NUT BREAD

Yield: 12 loaves, 9-inch by 5-inch

Ingredients

FLOUR, CAKE	6-1/4 pounds
SUGAR, BROWN	5 pounds
BUTTER or MARGARINE	3/4 pound
SALT	1 ounce
BAKING POWDER	3 ounces
SODA	1 ounce
GINGER, GROUND	1 ounce
CLOVES, GROUND	1/2 ounce
NONFAT DRY MILK	10 ounces
NUTS, chopped	1-1/2 pounds
EGGS	1 pound, 14 ounces
SOUR MILK or BUTTERMILK	2 pounds, 13 ounces

Procedure

1. Combine flour, sugar, butter, salt, baking powder, soda, spices, dry milk and nuts in mixer bowl. Mix at low speed 5 minutes.
2. Add eggs; mix until smooth.
3. Add sour milk; mix until smooth.
4. Turn into 12 greased and lightly floured 9-inch by 5-inch by 3-inch loaf pans.
5. Bake in oven at 360°F. for about 1 hour or until done.

Biscuits and Sweet Rolls from Biscuit Dough

BISCUITS are at their appetizing best when just out of the oven, piping hot. The popular napkin-lined basket looks inviting and helps retain heat. For a more off-beat approach, you can present them to your patrons direct from the oven, still on the baking pan. Or, for buffet service, try baking biscuits in colored rectangular baking dishes or oven-glass pie plates. Display them on the table just as they come from the oven, in the heat-holding baking dish.

The range of approaches to biscuit preparation offers one of the best ways to cope with breakfast monotony. You can introduce a seasoning or add ingredients such as grated orange rind, parsley, pimiento or cheese. You can put creativity in preparation to menu advantage at brunchtime by styling your biscuits to team with certain entrees. (But if you need biscuits to "go with everything," it's better to stay on neutral ground and stay with the plainer type.)

There's still more that you can do with biscuits by adding fruit, or a filling, to dress them up to appear as various sweet rolls and coffee cakes. Alternate proven combinations—brown sugar, cinnamon, dates, or similar blends—that provide flavorful fillings for pinwheels, crescents and other breakfast or cof-

fee hour treats. The classic three-cornered scone is another biscuit to feature that leans to the sweeter side. It's usually laced with currants or raisins and enriched with additional shortening and egg.

BAKING POWDER BISCUITS

Yield: approximately 220 biscuits

Ingredients
FLOUR, ALL-PURPOSE	8 pounds
SALT	3 ounces
BAKING POWDER	10 ounces
SHORTENING or MARGARINE	3 pounds
BUTTERMILK	1-1/2 quarts
MILK, WHOLE, SWEET	1-1/2 quarts
EGG YOLKS	3
MILK, WHOLE, SWEET	1 cup

Procedure

1. Place flour, salt and baking powder in mixing bowl. Add shortening; blend by hand or with pastry blender.
2. Add buttermilk and first amount of sweet milk alternately, a little at a time. Mix lightly until consistency is uniform throughout and a soft dough is formed.
3. Turn out on a floured board; roll 1/2-inch thick. Cut with a 2-inch biscuit cutter. Place on a greased, floured baking sheet.
4. Mix egg yolks and remaining milk. Brush tops of biscuits.
5. Bake in oven at 375°F. until done.

ICED DATE BISCUIT ROLLS

Yield: 48 rolls

Ingredients

DRIED DATE PIECES, medium	1 pound
SUGAR, GRANULATED	1 pound
WATER, hot	2 cups
PREPARED BISCUIT MIX	1 pound, 10 ounces
SUGAR, GRANULATED	1/3 cup
BUTTER or MARGARINE, melted	3 tablespoons
MILK	2 cups
CONFECTIONERS' SUGAR	8 ounces
MILK or WATER	1/4 cup
VANILLA or RUM FLAVORING	2 teaspoons

Procedure

1. Combine date pieces, first amount of sugar and hot water. Cook 10 minutes, stirring frequently. (Mixture should be thick but not stiff. It will get thicker as it cools.) Cool thoroughly.

2. Combine biscuit mix with remaining granulated sugar. Add melted butter and milk; mix until soft dough forms.

3. Turn out on a floured board. Divide into four equal portions (11-1/2 ounces each).

4. Roll each portion to a rectangular shape about 9-inches by 12-inches. Spread with 1/4 of the cooled filling. Roll up like cinnamon rolls, moistening the outer edge of dough to seal the roll.

5. Cut each roll into 12 uniform slices. Place in well-greased muffin pans. Bake in oven at 400°F. for 15 to 18 minutes, until rolls are golden brown. Remove from pans; cool slightly.

6. Combine confectioners' sugar, milk and flavoring; stir until smooth. Drizzle over rolls.

ORANGE PINWHEELS ━━━━▶

Yield: 96 1-1/2-ounce rolls

Ingredients
SUGAR	1 quart
ORANGE JUICE	1-1/2 quarts
BUTTER or MARGARINE	3/4 pound
ORANGE RIND, grated	3/4 cup
SUGAR	1-1/2 cups
CINNAMON	2 tablespoons
BAKING POWDER BISCUIT DOUGH	10 pounds

APPLE ROLL-UPS

Yield: 6 dozen

Ingredients
SUGAR	1/2 cup
BISCUIT MIX (PACKAGED)	2 quarts
EGGS, beaten	4
MILK	2 cups
APPLE SLICES, canned, coarsely chopped	2 quarts
SUGAR	1/2 cup
CINNAMON	4 teaspoons

Procedure

1. Add first amount of sugar to biscuit mix.
2. Combine eggs and milk; add to biscuit mix, mixing to form a soft dough.
3. Divide dough in 4 parts. Roll each portion into a strip 7-inch by 18-inch and 1/2-inch thick.
4. Spread 2 cups chopped apples on each strip; sprinkle with 2 tablespoons sugar and 1 teaspoon cinnamon.
5. Roll up lengthwise; seal edge. Cut each roll in 18 slices; place in paper-lined muffin pans.
6. Bake in oven at 425°F. for 15 minutes or until done. Serve warm.

Procedure
1. Combine first amount of sugar, orange juice, butter and grated orange rind; boil 3 minutes. Remove from heat; pour into two baking pans.
2. Mix remaining sugar and cinnamon.
3. Roll biscuit dough 1/2-inch thick. Sprinkle with cinnamon sugar mixture. Roll as for jelly roll, making a roll about 2 inches in diameter.
4. Cut in 1-inch slices; place in pans, flat side down, on top of orange mixture.
5. Bake in oven at 375°F. for 30 minutes or until done. Invert on cake racks at once. Serve warm.

QUICK APPLE SAUCE PINWHEELS

Yield: 90 to 96 pinwheels

Ingredients

CORNSTARCH	5-1/2 ounces (1-1/8 cups)
APPLE SAUCE	1 No. 10 can
BUTTER	6 ounces
HONEY	1-1/2 pounds (2 cups)
RAISINS	1 quart
BISCUIT MIX	6 pounds
SUGAR	1 cup
MILK	1-1/2 quarts
CINNAMON	as needed

Procedure
1. Blend cornstarch into apple sauce; add butter and honey. Heat; allow to boil 1 minute. Add raisins; cool.
2. Mix biscuit mix and sugar. Add milk; mix to form a soft dough.
3. Divide dough into eight 22-ounce portions. Roll each out into a rectangle 15-inches by 11-inches by 1/4-inch. Spread with 2 cups apple sauce filling. Sprinkle generously with cinnamon. Roll up jelly roll fashion. Cut in 1-inch slices.
4. Place slices close together in greased bun pan, cut side up. Bake in oven at 400°F. for 30 minutes or until done. Serve hot.

MAPLE RAISIN TWISTS

Yield: 5 dozen

Ingredients

FLOUR, ALL-PURPOSE	1 pound
SUGAR	1/2 cup
BAKING POWDER	2 tablespoons
SALT	2 teaspoons
SHORTENING	2/3 cup
RAISINS, DARK or GOLDEN	1-1/3 cups
EGGS, beaten	2
MILK	1 cup
BUTTER or MARGARINE, melted	1/4 pound
SUGAR, BROWN	4 ounces (2/3 cup, packed)
MAPLE FLAVORING	1/2 teaspoon
BUTTER or MARGARINE, melted	as needed

Procedure

1. Sift flour, sugar, baking powder and salt together.
2. Cut in shortening until mixture resembles coarse meal. Mix in raisins lightly.
3. Combine eggs and milk. Add to dry ingredients; mix to form soft dough.
4. Turn out on floured board. Turn dough over several times to flour surface lightly.
5. Divide dough in four parts. Roll each to 5-inch by 12-inch rectangle, 1/2-inch thick.
6. Mix first amount of melted butter, brown sugar and maple flavoring; spread lengthwise down half of each strip.
7. Fold plain side over sugar mixture. Roll lightly across to make folded strip about 3 inches wide. Cut 3/4-inch strips.
8. Place strips on lightly-greased baking sheet. Carefully make one or two twists in each strip; press ends lightly onto sheet to hold strips in place. Brush with melted butter.
9. Bake in oven at 400°F. for 10 to 12 minutes. Cool on wire rack. Brush with a confectioners' sugar glaze, if desired.

Yeast Rolls

Danish Builds Coffee Break Business

California Almond Growers Exchange

GLAZED ORANGE ROLLS

Yield: 48 rolls

Ingredients

SALT	1-1/2 teaspoons
SUGAR	3/4 cup
SHORTENING	6 ounces
SKIM MILK POWDER	1/3 cup
EGG, WHOLE, LARGE	1 (2-1/2 ounces)
EGG YOLKS	3 to 4 (2-1/2 ounces)
YEAST, BAKERS	
or YEAST, DRY or COMPRESSED	3 cakes or packages
WATER, lukewarm	1-1/2 cups
FLOUR, ALL-PURPOSE	1-3/4 to 2 pounds
BUTTER or MARGARINE	1/2 pound
SUGAR	2 cups
FROZEN ORANGE CONCENTRATE, thawed to room temperature	3 ounces (6 tablespoons)
CINNAMON-SUGAR MIXTURE	as needed
NUT MEATS, chopped (optional)	as needed

Procedure

1. Mix salt, sugar, shortening and skim milk powder on low speed until blended. Add eggs; mix well.

2. Dissolve yeast in water; add to creamed mixture; mix well.

3. Add flour on low speed; mix until blended. Knead on floured board until satiny. Place in a greased bowl. Cover; let rise until double in bulk.

4. Cream butter and sugar with orange concentrate until fluffy.

5. Divide dough into 4 pieces; roll each into rectangle 12-inches by 8-inches. Spread each piece with about 2 tablespoons of the orange mixture.

6. Sprinkle with a cinnamon-sugar mixture. Add a sprinkling of chopped nuts, if desired. Roll up like jelly roll; cut in 1-inch pieces.

7. Coat 2-1/2 inch muffin pans with orange mixture. Place rolls, cut side down, in pans; let rise until double in bulk.

8. Bake in oven at 375°F. for 20 minutes or until done. Invert pans as soon as removed from oven to prevent glaze from sticking to pan.

CINNAMON TWIST BREAD

Yield: 6 loaves

Ingredients

YEAST, DRY or COMPRESSED	6 packages or cakes
WATER, lukewarm	1 cup
MILK, scalded	4-1/2 cups
SUGAR	1-1/2 cups
SALT	2 tablespoons
SHORTENING	1 cup
FLOUR, sifted	4-1/2 to 5 pounds
EGGS, beaten	4
DRIED CURRANTS	3 cups
ROLLED OATS, QUICK or OLD-FASHIONED, uncooked	1 quart
CINNAMON	1/3 cup
SUGAR	1 cup

Procedure

1. Soften yeast in lukewarm water. (Use warm water for dry yeast.)
2. Pour scalded milk over sugar, salt and shortening. Cool to lukewarm.
3. Add half of flour, beaten eggs, softened yeast, currants and oats. Beat until blended.
4. Add enough flour to make a stiff dough. Mix with bread hook or knead until satiny, about 10 minutes.
5. Cover; let rise until doubled in size, about 1 hour.
6. Punch down; cover and let rest 10 minutes.
7. Divide dough into 6 equal parts (about 1 pound, 14 ounces each). Roll out each part to form a rectangle about 8-inches by 15-inches.
8. Combine cinnamon and sugar. Sprinkle part of mixture over rectangle of dough. Roll up to form a loaf; place with seam underneath in lightly-greased bread pan (1 pound size).
9. Brush loaves lightly with melted shortening; cover and let rise until almost doubled in size, about 45 minutes.
10. Bake in oven at 400°F. for 10 minutes. Reduce heat to 350°F. and continue baking 35 to 45 minutes until bread is brown and begins to leave sides of pan.

OATMEAL YEAST RAISED ROLLS ⟶

Yield: 12 dozen rolls

Ingredients
WATER, boiling	1-1/2 quarts
SHORTENING	12 ounces
ROLLED OATS	11 ounces (1 quart)
SUGAR, BROWN	12 ounces
SALT	3 tablespoons
EGGS, beaten	8 ounces (1 cup)
COMPRESSED YEAST	2-1/2 ounces
NONFAT DRY MILK	12 ounces
FLOUR	4-1/2 to 5 pounds

RAISIN CHEESE BUNS

Yield: approximately 8 dozen

Ingredients
CREAM CHEESE	2 pounds, 12 ounces
LEMON JUICE	1/3 cup
MILK	1-1/2 cups
RAISINS, SEEDLESS	4 pounds, 4 ounces
BASIC SWEET DOUGH	9 pounds
EGG WASH or BUTTER, melted	as needed

Procedure
1. Beat cheese with lemon juice until smooth and creamy.
2. Blend in milk and raisins.
3. Roll dough 3/8-inch thick. Cut into 2-1/2-inch to 3-1/2-inch squares.
4. Put about 1 ounce filling in center of each square. Bring corners of squares to center; pinch together firmly. Place on greased baking sheets.
5. Brush with egg wash or melted butter.
6. Proof until doubled in size, about 45 minutes.
7. Bake in oven at 400°F. for 10 to 15 minutes or until done.

Procedure

1. Pour boiling water over shortening, rolled oats, brown sugar and salt. Let stand until lukewarm.

2. Add beaten eggs and crumbled yeast; blend

3. Sift nonfat dry milk with 2 pounds of the flour. Add to yeast mixture; beat until smooth.

4. Add enough flour to make a soft dough. Knead. Let stand until doubled in bulk (about 1 hour).

5. Punch down. Let rest 10 minutes. Shape into 1-1/2-inch balls.

6. Place in greased pans. Brush with melted shortening. Cover; let rise 45 minutes.

7. Bake in oven at 375°F. for 20 to 25 minutes.

CHEESE ROLLS

Yield: approximately 10 dozen

Ingredients

HOT ROLL MIX	5 pounds
WATER, warm	2-1/2 pounds
BUTTER or MARGARINE, melted	as needed
CHEESE, AMERICAN, grated	2 pounds

Procedure

1. Mix dough according to package directions. Allow dough to rise until doubled in size.

2. Divide dough in half. Roll each half to about 1/4-inch thickness. Brush with melted butter or margarine. Sprinkle with grated cheese.

3. Roll up as for cinnamon rolls. Cut into rolls of desired size (average size is approximately 1-1/4 ounces). Place, cut side down, in greased muffin pans. Proof until rolls are about double in size.

4. Bake in oven at 400°F. for 12 to 15 minutes. Immediately after taking rolls from oven, brush tops with melted butter or margarine.

PARISIENNE BRIOCHES

Yield: 6 to 7 dozen

Ingredients

YEAST	1-1/2 ounces
MILK, lukewarm	1/2 cup
FLOUR, BREAD	2-1/2 pounds
EGGS, MEDIUM	12
SALT	1 tablespoon
SUGAR	6 ounces
BUTTER, soft	1 pound, 10 ounces
EGG, beaten	as needed
WATER	as needed

Procedure

1. Soften yeast in milk; add about 8 ounces of flour to make a soft dough. Place in a mixer bowl; cover with remaining flour; let rise in a warm place for 1 hour.

2. Add eggs; beat at moderate speed until all ingredients are blended. If dough is too stiff, increase the eggs.

3. Beat on high speed until mixture slips the bowl and the paddle (approximately 5 minutes).

4. Change machine to lower speed. Add butter all at one time. Do not over-mix. The dough and butter should just be mixed thoroughly.

5. Let dough rise until doubled in bulk. Punch down. Refrigerate overnight.

6. Shape in two parts—the main part of the brioche, and the small ball for the "top knot" on top. Place in small brioche or muffin pans.

7. Let rise. Before baking, brush with beaten egg mixed with a small amount of water. Bake in oven at 375°F.

CHERRY-FILLED BREAKFAST BREAD

Yield: 4 breads—48 portions

Ingredients

ACTIVE DRY YEAST	1 ounce
WATER, warm	2 cups
EGGS, slightly beaten	4
BISCUIT MIX	2-1/2 quarts
BUTTER or MARGARINE, soft	1 pound
SUGAR, BROWN	1 pound
CINNAMON	1-1/2 teaspoons
SALT	1 teaspoon
WALNUTS or PECANS, chopped	1 pound
CHERRIES, CANDIED, chopped	1 quart

Procedure

1. Soften yeast in warm water.
2. Add eggs and biscuit mix; beat well.
3. Turn out on floured board; knead until smooth, about 20 strokes.
4. Divide dough into 8 equal portions. Roll each to a rectangle 12-inch by 7-inch. Place 4 of the rectangles on greased baking sheets.
5. Combine butter, brown sugar, cinnamon and salt. Add nuts and cherries.
6. Sprinkle fruit mixture over rectangles on baking sheets. Place remaining 4 rectangles on top of filling.
7. Cover; let rise until doubled in bulk.
8. Bake in oven at 400°F. for 12 to 15 minutes or until done. Finish top with a glaze, if desired.

FILLED SWEET ROLLS

Yield: approximately 48 3-inch rolls

Ingredients

YEAST	2 ounces
WATER, lukewarm (85°F.)	1 cup
MILK	1-1/2 cups
SUGAR	1 cup
SALT	2 tablespoons
SHORTENING	1/2 cup
FLOUR, ALL-PURPOSE	2-3/4 quarts (about)
EGGS, beaten	4

Procedure

1. Soften yeast in lukewarm water. Scald milk; add sugar, salt and shortening. Cool to lukewarm.

2. Add 1 quart flour; mix well. Add softened yeast and beaten eggs; mix well.

3. Add remaining flour to make a moderately soft dough. Knead or mix until smooth and satiny.

4. Place in lightly-greased bowl. Grease surface of dough lightly. Cover; let rise in warm place (85°F.) until doubled in bulk (about 2-1/2 hours).

5. When dough is light, punch down; divide into 2 equal portions. Cover; let rest 10 to 15 minutes.

6. Roll out each portion to long narrow sheet about 8 inches wide and 1/4 inch thick. Spread 1-1/4 to 1-1/2 cups filling* on each portion. Roll up like jelly-roll. Cut into 1-inch slices. Place, cut side down, into greased 3-inch muffin pans.

7. Brush with milk; sprinkle lightly with sugar. Let rise until doubled in bulk (about 3/4 hour).

8. Bake in oven at 375°F. for 20 to 25 minutes.

*See Apple Raisin Filling, page 222, Prune Filling, page 227.

DANISH PASTRY
(Average richness)

Yield: 22 pounds, 11 ounces dough

Ingredients	
SUGAR	1-1/4 pounds
SALT	3 ounces
NONFAT DRY MILK SOLIDS	8 ounces
FLAVOR	as desired
SHORTENING (SPECIAL FOR SWEET ROLLS)	1 pound
EGGS	2 pounds
WATER	2 quarts
YEAST	12 ounces
FLOUR, BREAD	6 pounds
FLOUR, PASTRY	3 pounds
MARGARINE (SPECIAL FOR ROLL-IN)	4 pounds

Procedure

1. Cream sugar, salt, nonfat milk solids, flavor and shortening until smooth. Add eggs; cream smooth.

2. Combine water and yeast; dissolve. Add to creamed mixture.

3. Sift flours; add to mixture; mix until smooth. (Dough temperature from mixer $50°$ to $60°F$.)

4. Fold dough into an oblong; let rest in refrigerator until pliable.

5. Roll dough into a rectangular sheet about 3/4 inch thick. Spot or spread roll-in margarine over 2/3 of the surface. Fold uncovered portion to center of covered portion; fold again, making two layers of margarine within three layers of dough.

6. Roll again to about 1/2 inch thickness and fold in 3 layers. Again let dough rest until pliable.

7. Repeat rolling and folding, making a total of three rolls.

8. Make up into units. Proof at $90°F$.

9. Bake small units at $390°$ to $400°F$., larger units (10 to 16 ounces) at $360°$ to $370°F$. Glaze and frost while still warm.

RICH DANISH PASTRY

Yield: approximately 12 pounds dough

Ingredients
SUGAR	12 ounces
SHORTENING, ALL-PURPOSE YEAST DOUGH	12 ounces
SALT	1-3/4 ounces
SPICE	as desired
FLOUR, BREAD	3 pounds
FLOUR, PASTRY	1-1/2 pounds
NONFAT DRY MILK	4 ounces
EGGS, WHOLE	1 pound
WATER (VARIABLE)	2 pounds
YEAST	8 ounces
FLAVOR	as desired
SHORTENING, ALL-PURPOSE YEAST DOUGH	2-1/2 pounds

Procedure

1. Place sugar, first amount of all-purpose yeast dough shortening, salt, spice, flours and nonfat dry milk in mixing bowl.

2. At medium speed, add eggs and water in which yeast has been dissolved. Add flavor. Continue mixing to a dough (3 to 4 minutes mixing).

3. Bring dough from mixer at 75°F. Let the dough loosen up on the bench. Roll in the second amount of all-purpose yeast dough shortening, giving the dough 3 rolls, 3 folds each.

4. Place in a cold retarder or freezer for several hours, or preferably overnight.

5. Make up into the desired pieces (if frozen, allow 1/2 hour to loosen up slightly).

6. Proof until pieces are about double in size.

7. Bake in oven at 400°F.

8. While still hot, glaze with a corn syrup glaze (1 quart of corn syrup, 1 quart water brought to a boil). Ice and garnish with nut meats, coconut or various toppings, if desired.

DANISH PASTRY
(Using sweet roll mix)

Yield: 15 10-ounce coffee cakes, or 115 1-1/4 ounce rolls

Ingredients

SWEET ROLL MIX (DRY)	5 pounds
WATER, heated to 110°F.	2 cups
YEAST (from mix)	both packets
WATER, cold (from tap)	2 cups
BUTTER or BUTTER BLENDED WITH MARGARINE	1 pound, 5 ounces to 2 pounds, 10 ounces

Procedure

1. Place sweet roll mix in mixer bowl.
2. Combine warm water and yeast; stir to dissolve.
3. Pour cold water in bowl with mix. Add yeast solution; mix at low speed for 1 to 1-1/2 minutes or until dough is smooth. (Dough temperature 60° to 70°F.)
4. Place dough on bench directly from mixer. Form dough into oblong strips. Place on a floured sheet pan. Cover with wax paper or damp cloth. Put in dough retarder at 34° to 38°F., 85% humidity. Allow to remain in retarder at least 30 minutes.
5. Roll out into rectangular shape 1/4-inch to 3/8-inch thick.
6. Dot 2/3 of the length of dough with butter, working from the top down. (Use butter according to richness desired.)
7. Fold uncovered 1/3 of dough to center of covered portion; fold again, making two layers of butter within three layers of dough.
8. Turn folded sheet lengthwise; roll out to original size. Fold as before *adding no butter* this time.
9. Place dough on sheet pan, cover, return to retarder for 20 to 30 minutes to relax.
10. Repeat rolling and folding. (This makes three rollings and folds.) Return to retarder for 15 to 20 minutes to relax.
11. Divide dough; make up into coffee cakes or rolls, as desired.
12. Proof at 80°F. Bake in oven at 400°F. until golden brown (approximately 15 minutes). Glaze while hot; finish by icing.

Note

Five pounds mix makes 7 pounds dough. When making larger batches scale dough into 7 pound units for convenient handling.

Fruit-Sparked Kuchens for Coffee Breaks

Pillsbury Food Service

Kuchens

KUCHENS and similar coffee cakes are usually made with a muffin-like batter that is baked in a pan. They lend themselves to streusel, spiced sugar or chopped nut toppings, and to taste-tempting additions of fruit. Apples, dates, raisins, and blueberries are but a few of the additions that increase orders.

These quick breads, like others that are baked as a sheet, have a quick portioning advantage—all that is needed is to cut them into squares of the designated size.

CRANBERRY KUCHEN

Yield: 50 2-1/2-inch squares

Ingredients

SUGAR	3/4 cup
CRANBERRIES, FRESH, coarsely ground	1-1/2 pounds
FLOUR, CAKE	2 pounds, 10 ounces
SUGAR	1 pound, 5 ounces
BAKING POWDER	1/4 cup
SALT	1-1/2 tablespoons
SHORTENING	1 pound, 2 ounces
EGGS, beaten	10 ounces (6 eggs)
MILK	3 cups
SUGAR	7 ounces
ORANGE RIND, grated	1 tablespoon
CINNAMON	1 teaspoon

Procedure

1. Add first amount of sugar to cranberries; let stand 10 minutes.
2. Combine flour, next amount of sugar, baking powder and salt in mixer bowl. Blend at low speed, using pastry cutter or flat beater (about 1 minute).
3. Add shortening to dry mixture; continue blending until mixture resembles coarse crumbs (about 2 minutes).
4. Combine beaten eggs and milk; blend into flour mixture.
5. Add cranberries to batter; mix only enough to distribute well.
6. Turn into greased shallow pans to depth of 1/2 inch.
7. Combine remaining sugar, orange rind and cinnamon; mix well. Sprinkle topping over batter.
8. Bake in oven at 350°F. for 30 to 35 minutes or until done.
9. Cut into squares. Serve hot.

Variations

Cherry Kuchen—substitute 3 cups chopped, well-drained sweetened frozen red cherries for first amount of sugar and cranberries.

Cranberry-Orange Kuchen—omit first amount of sugar and cranberries. Spread batter in pans, then swirl 2 cups canned cranberry-orange relish into batter. Sprinkle with topping; bake as directed.

Almond Kuchen—omit first amount of sugar and cranberries. Spread batter in pans; sprinkle with 2 cups chopped almonds and the topping. Bake as directed.

QUICK PRUNE-ORANGE KUCHEN

Yield: 24 portions

Ingredients	
PRUNES	1-1/2 pounds
WATER	3 cups
SHORTENING	5 ounces (2/3 cup)
SUGAR, GRANULATED	10 ounces (1-1/3 cups)
EGGS	5-1/2 ounces (2/3 cup)
MILK	1-1/4 cups
ORANGE RIND, grated	1 tablespoon
FLOUR, ALL-PURPOSE	1 pound
BAKING POWDER	1-1/2 tablespoons
SALT	1-1/2 teaspoons
TOPPING	
FLOUR, ALL-PURPOSE	1/4 cup
SUGAR, BROWN	1 cup (packed)
CINNAMON	2 teaspoons
BUTTER	1/4 cup
ORANGE RIND, grated	1 teaspoon

Procedure

1. Cover prunes with water. Simmer 20 minutes. Cool to handle. Drain; remove pits.
2. Cream shortening and sugar.
3. Beat in eggs. Blend in milk and orange rind.
4. Sift flour, baking powder and salt together. Add to creamed mixture; mix to blend.
5. Turn into greased 12-inch by 20-inch by 2-1/2-inch baking pan. Arrange prunes on top of batter.
6. Combine topping ingredients. Sprinkle over top of batter.
7. Bake in oven at 375°F. for 30 minutes or until done. Cool; cut in squares.

Holiday Assortment of Breakfast Breads

Pillsbury Food Service

BLUEBERRY OR APPLE KUCHEN

Yield: 68 2-ounce portions

Ingredients

FLOUR, CAKE	2 pounds, 10 ounces
BAKING POWDER	1-1/2 ounces (3-3/4 tablespoons)
SALT	1-1/2 tablespoons
SUGAR	1 pound, 5 ounces
NUTMEG	3/4 teaspoon
SHORTENING	1 pound, 2 ounces
EGGS, well-beaten	6 (10 ounces)
MILK	3 cups
BLUEBERRIES, FRESH or FROZEN* or APPLES, finely chopped	1 quart
SUGAR	4 ounces
CINNAMON	3/4 teaspoon

Procedure

1. Sift cake flour, baking powder, salt, sugar and nutmeg together twice. Cut in shortening.
2. Combine eggs and milk. Add to flour mixture; blend. Fold in fruit.
3. Turn into greased shallow pans, making a 3/4-inch layer.
4. Mix sugar and cinnamon together; sprinkle over batter.
5. Bake in oven at 350°F. for 20 to 25 minutes. Cut in squares. Serve hot.

*Use unthawed frozen blueberries.

200 BREAKFAST AND BRUNCH DISHES

Louisiana Crullers (See recipe, p. 207)

Louisiana Yam Commission

Doughnuts

DOUGHNUTS ARE BELOVED by Americans everywhere. There's something comforting and friendly about this homey treat that lends a certain charm and sets it a little apart from other traditional fare.

    Perhaps no other food is quite as quick to stir a childhood memory—of Mother in the kitchen—the family breakfast table—a heartening pot of coffee—the teasing smell of spice. Perhaps nothing can do quite as much to mark your breakfast as "special" as an offering of freshly prepared doughnuts with the fragrance that asserts their gentle warmth.

    Generally speaking, doughnuts are small, sweet cakes, cut into circles with a hole in the center and fried in deep fat. They are made either with a dough that is leavened with yeast or with a stiff cake-like dough that contains baking powder and, frequently, spice as well.

    The classic yeast-made doughnut is either left plain, rolled in granulated sugar or finished with a thin glaze. The cake-like types are traditionally either plain or rolled in sugar (confectioners' or granulated) or in a mixture of sugar and cinnamon. New and imaginative treatments include dressing up the cake-like doughnuts by slicing into halves, then spreading with a mixture boasting sugar and nuts before toasting in the oven and serving forth hot.

Crullers and fried cakes are akin to the doughnut clan. The cruller is, properly, a fried product fashioned from strips of dough twisted together. The distinguishing feature is the shape, for the dough can be either the yeast or baking powder type.

French crullers, though, are quite different. They are made from a cream puff (choux paste) batter, forced through a pastry tube into a circular, ring-like shape. They are fried in deep fat and are often sprinkled lightly with confectioners' sugar or brushed with a glaze.

Fried cakes (or fried bread or doughboys) are made of yeast dough cut into strips, rounds, squares or diamond-shaped pieces and fried like doughnuts. They are sometimes eaten as a hot bread or served with syrup as a breakfast or dessert item. Again, they are sometimes cooled and coated with icing.

Names, however, don't mean the same thing in all communities. In some parts of the country doughnuts are known as "fried cakes." In some places the name fried cakes applies to doughnuts and crullers as well as to the fried yeast-leavened product made without holes. To add to the confusion, the filled items which one might expect to call fried cakes (since they don't have holes) are, contrary to the rule, sometimes known as doughnuts. Jelly doughnuts are a case in point. In turn, jelly doughnuts go by the name "Bismarcks" in parts of the Middle West!

SHERRY PUFF BALLS

Yield: approximately 5 dozen small puffs

Ingredients

EGGS	4
SUGAR	1 cup
ORANGE RIND, grated	2 tablespoons
SHORTENING, soft	1/4 cup
FLOUR, ALL-PURPOSE	1 pound
BAKING POWDER	4 teaspoons
SALT	2 teaspoons
SHERRY WINE	1/2 cup
ORANGE JUICE	1/2 cup
FAT FOR FRYING	

Procedure

1. Beat eggs until light and foamy; beat in sugar, orange rind and shortening.

2. Sift flour, baking powder and salt together. Add to egg mixture alternately with sherry and orange juice, blending until smooth after each addition.

3. Drop by teaspoonsful into hot fat (375°F.). (Dip spoon in fat first to allow dough to slide off easily.) Fry about 2 minutes, turning to brown evenly. Drain on paper toweling. Dip while still hot into Sherry Glaze.*

*SHERRY GLAZE

Ingredients

SUGAR, CONFECTIONERS', sifted	2 cups
SHERRY WINE	1/4 cup

Procedure

1. Combine ingredients, blend until smooth.

PRALINE DOUGHNUTS

Yield: approximately 17 dozen

Ingredients

SUGAR, BROWN	1 pound
SHORTENING, HIGH RATIO LIQUID or HIGH RATIO SOLID	1-1/2 pounds
SALT	2 ounces
NUTMEG	1/8 ounce
MACE	1/8 ounce
FLOUR, BREAD	4 pounds
FLOUR, PASTRY	4 pounds
BAKING POWDER	2-1/2 ounces
NONFAT DRY MILK	1/2 pound
WATER (variable)	4 pounds
YEAST	10 ounces
EGGS, WHOLE	1 pound
PECANS, coarsely chopped	1-1/2 pounds

Procedure

1. Place sugar, shortening, salt, spices, flours, baking powder and dry milk powder in mixer bowl.

2. Combine water and yeast; blend.

3. With mixer at medium speed, add eggs and yeast mixture. Continue mixing to a smooth dough, 8 to 10 minutes.

4. Bring the dough from the mixer at 78° to 85°F. Let rest 20 minutes.

5. Roll out to 1/2 inch thickness. Cut out doughnuts.

6. Proof about 30 minutes or until 3/4 proofed.

7. Fry doughnuts (scaled 16 ounces per dozen) in deep fat at 365° to 375°F.

8. Glaze with praline icing. (Recipe facing page.)

PRALINE ICING

Yield: 9-1/2 pounds

Ingredients

SUGAR, BROWN	2 pounds
GLUCOSE	1 pound
WATER	1 pound
SALT	1/4 ounce
SUGAR, CONFECTIONERS'	5 pounds
PECANS, finely chopped	8 ounces

Procedure

1. Combine brown sugar, glucose, water and salt; bring to a boil.
2. Pour hot syrup over confectioners' sugar; stir until smooth. Add pecans.

Note

If icing becomes thick, thin down with simple syrup made by combining 2 pounds granulated sugar with 1 pound water; bring to a boil; cool.

WHITE FROSTING

Yield: for 8 dozen doughnuts

Ingredients

BUTTER or MARGARINE, softened	2 tablespoons
SUGAR, CONFECTIONERS'	1 pound
CORN SYRUP, LIGHT	1 tablespoon
VANILLA EXTRACT	1 teaspoon
WATER, hot	3 tablespoons (about)

Procedure

1. Cream butter. Add sugar, syrup and vanilla.
2. Add hot water as needed, beating to smooth, creamy consistency.

Variations

1. Add 1/2 cup cocoa, blending with confectioners' sugar.
2. Add 1/8 teaspoon ground cloves along with the cocoa.
3. Sprinkle tops of doughnuts (spread with white icing) with toasted sesame seeds.

TASTY RICH YEAST-RAISED DOUGHNUTS

Yield: 8 dozen

Ingredients

SUGAR	9-1/2 ounces
SHORTENING, HIGH RATIO	12 ounces
SALT	1 ounce
MACE	1/4 ounce
NUTMEG	1/4 ounce
FLOUR, BREAD	2 pounds
FLOUR, PASTRY	1 pound, 12 ounces
BAKING POWDER	1-1/4 ounces
NONFAT DRY MILK POWDER	4 ounces
WATER	2 pounds
YEAST	5 ounces
EGGS, WHOLE	8 ounces

Procedure

1. Place sugar, shortening, salt, spices, flours, baking powder and dry milk in mixing bowl.
2. Combine water and yeast, stirring to dissolve.
3. With mixer at medium speed, add eggs and yeast mixture. Continue mixing to a smooth dough, about 2 to 3 minutes. (Temperature 78° to 85°F.)
4. Let dough rest about 20 minutes before make-up.
5. Roll and cut doughnuts, scaling 12 to a pound.
6. Proof about 20 minutes. Do not overproof.
7. Fry in hot deep fat at 375°F.
8. If desired, glaze with Honey Doughnut Glaze (recipe p. 208) while doughnuts are piping hot.

Note

A convenient way to handle glazing is to dip the hot doughnuts in the glaze while on the wire screen and then allow them to remain on the screen until glaze sets up.

LOUISIANA CRULLERS
(See picture, p. 200)

Yield: approximately 14 dozen

Ingredients

EGGS	18
SUGAR	3-1/2 pounds
VANILLA	1-1/2 tablespoons
YAMS, cooked, mashed*	3 pounds
COOKING OIL or SHORTENING, melted	5 ounces
FLOUR, ALL-PURPOSE	6 pounds
BAKING POWDER	2/3 cup
SALT	2 tablespoons
CINNAMON	1-1/2 to 2 tablespoons
NUTMEG	1-1/2 to 2 tablespoons
CLOVES, GROUND	2 teaspoons
MILK	3 cups

Procedure

1. Beat eggs; add sugar; beat until light. Add vanilla.
2. Add yams and oil; mix well.
3. Sift flour, baking powder, salt and spices. Add to yam mixture alternately with milk, mixing well after each addition.
4. Chill dough thoroughly, at least 3 hours.
5. Roll out a small amount of dough at a time, rolling to rectangles about 1/2 inch thick. Cut 1 inch wide, 8 inches long. Fold strips in half lengthwise and twist. Chill 15 minutes.
6. Fry in deep fat at 375°F. turning once, until nicely browned.
7. Drain; roll in granulated sugar.

*Fresh, canned, frozen or instant flakes.

HONEY DOUGHNUT GLAZE

Yield: approximately 12-3/4 pounds

Ingredients
WATER	2-1/4 pounds
HONEY	1/2 pound
GELATINE	1 ounce
SUGAR, CONFECTIONERS'	10 pounds
SALT	1/2 ounce
FLAVOR	to taste

Procedure

1. Combine water and honey; mix. Sprinkle gelatine on top to soften. Bring to a boil.

2. Combine sugar and salt. Add hot gelatine mixture; stir until smooth. Flavor to taste.

TOASTED CINNAMON-PECAN DOUGHNUTS

Yield: 48 portions, 2 halves each

Ingredients
BUTTER or MARGARINE, soft	1/2 pound
SUGAR, BROWN, firmly packed	1 cup (6 ounces)
CINNAMON, GROUND	2 teaspoons
PECANS, finely chopped	1 cup
DOUGHNUTS, PLAIN	48

Procedure

1. Combine butter, sugar, cinnamon and pecans.

2. Slice doughnuts in half, crosswise. Spread about half a tablespoon mixture on cut side of each doughnut half.

3. Place on bun pans (18-inch by 26-inch by 1-inch) and toast, as needed, in oven at 400°F. for about 5 minutes. Serve hot.

MAPLE-NUT DOUGHNUTS

Yield: 48 portions, 2 halves each

Ingredients

BUTTER or MARGARINE, soft	3/4 pound
MAPLE SYRUP	3/4 cup
PECANS, finely chopped	3 cups
DOUGHNUTS, PLAIN	48

Procedure
1. Combine butter, maple syrup and pecans.
2. Slice doughnuts in half, crosswise.
3. Spread about 2 teaspoons of the maple-nut mixture on cut side of each doughnut half.
4. Place on bun pans (18-inch by 26-inch by 1-inch) and toast in oven at 400°F. for about 10 minutes.

LEMON-COCONUT DOUGHNUTS

Yield: 48 portions, 2 halves each

Ingredients

SUGAR, GRANULATED	3 cups
LEMON RIND, grated	1/4 cup
LEMON JUICE	3/4 cup
DOUGHNUTS, PLAIN	48
COCONUT, SHREDDED or FLAKED	3 cups (1/2 pound)

Procedure
1. Combine sugar, lemon rind and lemon juice.
2. Slice doughnuts in half, crosswise.
3. Spread about a teaspoon of lemon mixture over cut side of each doughnut half. Sprinkle with coconut.
4. Place on bun pans (18-inch by 26-inch by 1-inch) and toast in oven at 400°F. for about 10 minutes.

SPICED DOUGHNUTS

Yield: approximately 8 dozen

Ingredients

SUGAR	1-1/4 pounds
SALT	1 tablespoon
CINNAMON, GROUND	2 teaspoons
NUTMEG, GROUND	2 teaspoons
SHORTENING	3/4 cup
EGGS	8
VANILLA EXTRACT	4 teaspoons
FLOUR, ALL-PURPOSE	3-1/2 pounds (3-1/2 quarts)
BAKING POWDER	1/3 cup
MILK	1 quart
SUGGESTIONS FOR SPICING	
POPPY SEED	1/2 cup
SESAME SEED, TOASTED	1/2 cup
APPLE PIE SPICE	1/4 cup
NUTMEG, GROUND	1 tablespoon
CINNAMON, GROUND	1 tablespoon
ALLSPICE, GROUND	2 teaspoons
GINGER, GROUND	2 teaspoons

Procedure

1. Mix sugar, salt and spices. Add shortening; cream well.
2. Add eggs, a few at a time; blend well after each addition. Add vanilla; blend.
3. Sift flour with baking powder. Add to egg mixture alternately with milk, blending until smooth. Do not overmix.
4. Roll on lightly floured board to 1/2 inch thickness. Cut with a 2-1/2 inch round doughnut cutter. Remove centers. Re-roll centers and trimmings with any remaining dough.
5. Fry doughnuts in deep fat at 375°F. until lightly browned, turning once.
6. Drain on absorbent paper.
7. Roll slightly cooled doughnuts in cinnamon sugar (mixture of 1 pound granulated sugar, 3 tablespoons ground cinnamon) or, dust with confectioners' sugar, if desired.

Spice Variations

In place of the 2 teaspoons cinnamon and the 2 teaspoons of nutmeg in recipe on facing page use one of the suggestions for spicing.

Whole Wheat Variation

Use equal parts (by measure) of whole wheat and all-purpose flours. Spice as desired.

Yam Doughnuts, Scones Add New Menu Interest

Louisiana Yam Commission

Scones · Gingerbread · Popovers · Sally Lunn

POPOVERS

Yield: 5 dozen

Ingredients
FLOUR, ALL-PURPOSE	1 pound, 12 ounces
SALT	1 tablespoon
MILK	3 pounds, 14 ounces
EGGS	14

Procedure
1. Combine ingredients; mix on medium speed until smooth.
2. Pour into well-greased deep muffin pans, filling cups 3/4 full.
3. Bake in oven at 425°F. for 40 to 45 minutes or until done. Serve at once.

RAISIN SCONES

Yield: 24 large

Ingredients

RAISINS, LIGHT or DARK	1-1/2 cups
FLOUR, ALL-PURPOSE	1 pound
SALT	2 teaspoons
BAKING POWDER	2 tablespoons
SUGAR	1 cup
SHORTENING	1 cup (7 ounces)
EGGS	2
MILK	as needed
SUGAR	as needed

Procedure

1. Rinse raisins; drain.
2. Sift flour with salt, baking powder and first amount of sugar. Cut in shortening. Add raisins.
3. Beat eggs lightly; add enough milk to make 1-1/2 cups. Add to dry mixture; mix until soft dough is formed.
4. Turn out onto lightly floured board; knead lightly.
5. Divide dough into 6 equal parts. Pat or roll each to 6-inch circle.
6. Cut each circle of dough into 4 wedges. Place on greased baking sheet. Brush tops with milk; sprinkle with sugar.
7. Bake in oven at 425°F. for about 15 minutes or until well-browned. Serve hot.

YAM SCONES

Yield: 12 dozen

Ingredients	
FLOUR	7-1/2 pounds
SUGAR	11 ounces
BAKING POWDER	3/4 cup
SALT	2 tablespoons
SHORTENING	1 pound, 10 ounces
YAMS, cooked, mashed	4-1/2 pounds
EGGS, beaten	24 (5 cups)
MILK	1-1/2 cups
CURRANTS	1 pound, 5 ounces
MILK	as needed
SUGAR	as needed

Procedure

1. Combine flour, first amount of sugar, baking powder and salt. Sift.
2. Cut in shortening. Add yams.
3. Combine eggs, first amount of milk and currants. Add to flour mixture; mix until dough forms.
4. Turn out on floured board; knead 15 to 20 turns.
5. Roll out to 1/2 inch thickness, forming rectangle. Cut into 4-inch squares. Cut each square in half diagonally.
6. Arrange on greased baking sheets. Brush tops with milk, sprinkle with sugar.
7. Bake in oven at 425°F. for 12 minutes or until just lightly browned around sides.

GINGERBREAD

Yield: 9-1/4 pounds batter, 4 10-inch by 10-inch by 2-inch pans

Ingredients

FLOUR	2-1/2 pounds
BAKING POWDER	4 teaspoons
SALT	4 teaspoons
SODA	4 teaspoons
CINNAMON	4 teaspoons
CLOVES	4 teaspoons
GINGER	4 teaspoons
SHORTENING	14 ounces (2 cups)
SUGAR	14 ounces (2 cups)
EGGS, unbeaten	8
WATER	1 quart
MOLASSES	1 quart

Procedure

1. Sift flour, baking powder, salt, soda and spices together.
2. Cream shortening and sugar together thoroughly.
3. Add eggs, a few at a time; beat well after each addition.
4. Combine water and molasses.
5. Add dry ingredients to creamed mixture alternately with liquid, beating after each addition. (Mixture may curdle which does not affect quality of finished gingerbread.)
6. Turn batter into greased baking pans. Bake in oven at 350°F. for 40 to 45 minutes or until done. Serve warm.

QUICK SALLY LUNN

Yield: 6 pounds batter, 48 2-ounce portions

Ingredients

FLOUR, ALL-PURPOSE	1-3/4 pounds
BAKING POWDER	1/4 cup
SALT	2 teaspoons
NUTMEG	1 teaspoon
SHORTENING	7 ounces (1 cup)
SUGAR, GRANULATED	12 ounces (1-3/4 cups)
EGGS, WHOLE	13 ounces (1-1/2 cups)
MILK	3 cups
SUGAR, LIGHT BROWN	12 ounces (2 cups, packed measure)
CINNAMON	4 teaspoons
BUTTER, melted	2 ounces (1/4 cup)

Procedure

1. Sift flour, baking powder, salt and nutmeg together.
2. Cream shortening. Gradually blend in granulated sugar; cream together well.
3. Add eggs a few at a time, beating well after each addition.
4. Add sifted dry ingredients alternately with milk, blending after each addition until smooth.
5. Pour batter into four greased 9-inch by 9-inch by 2-inch baking pans.*
6. Mix brown sugar, cinnamon and butter; sprinkle over batter. Bake in oven at 350°F. for 25 to 30 minutes.

*Or use 2-inch deep round or rectangular pans. Pour batter to a depth of 1/2 inch. (Finished height of the Sally Lunn should be approximately 1-1/2 inches.)

Special Treatment

MUSHROOM MILK TOAST

Yield: 48 portions

Ingredients

CREAM OF MUSHROOM SOUP, CONDENSED	2-1/2 quarts
MILK	1 gallon
BUTTER or MARGARINE	3 tablespoons
ENRICHED BREAD TOAST	48 slices

Procedure

   1. Combine mushroom soup and milk; beat with a wire whip until blended. Heat; add butter.

   2. For each portion, place a slice of toast in flat soup dish; ladle 1/2 cup hot soup over it.

CINNAMON-ORANGE LOAF ⟶

Yield: 48 portions (3 slices each)

Ingredients	
BUTTER or MARGARINE, soft	1 pound
SUGAR, LIGHT BROWN	1-1/2 pounds
SUGAR, GRANULATED	1-1/2 pounds
CINNAMON	2 tablespoons
ORANGE JUICE*	1/2 cup
ORANGE RIND, grated (if desired)	1/4 cup
FRENCH BREAD, BROWN 'N SERVE	12 5-ounce loaves

APPLE-CINNAMON TOAST

Yield: 24 portions, 2 slices each

Ingredients	
ENRICHED BREAD SLICES	48
BUTTER or MARGARINE	1/4 pound
SUGAR, GRANULATED	1/2 cup
CINNAMON, GROUND	1 tablespoon
APPLESAUCE, UNSWEETENED	2 quarts

Procedure
1. Toast bread. Butter lightly allowing 1/2 teaspoon per slice.
2. Combine sugar and cinnamon; sprinkle over buttered toast.
3. Heat applesauce.
4. Spoon 1/3 cup hot applesauce over a slice of hot cinnamon toast. Cut another slice in half, diagonally; arrange over applesauce. Serve at once.

Note

If desired, place cinnamon toast, sugar side up, on ungreased bun pans. Heat in oven at 350°F. for 5 minutes just before adding applesauce layer and serving.

Procedure

1. Combine butter, sugars, cinnamon, orange juice and rind in a 2 quart mixing bowl.

2. Cut each loaf of bread diagonally, almost through to bottom crust, into 12 equal-sized slices.

3. Spread about 1-1/2 teaspoons cinnamon-orange butter on each slice of bread.

4. String each loaf on a sharp-pointed skewer, inserting the skewer through the center of each loaf.

5. Heat each loaf over hot coals, or under a broiler, turning so bread is browned on all sides.

*Fresh, canned, concentrated canned or frozen orange juice can be used. Use fresh or canned in natural strength and add grated rind for more flavor. Dilute concentrated canned or frozen by one-half usual proportions for added flavor.

LEMON ROLLS

Yield: 24

Ingredients

SUGAR, GRANULATED	3/4 cup
LEMON RIND, grated	2-1/2 teaspoons
LEMON JUICE	2-1/2 tablespoons
BUTTER or MARGARINE, soft	3 tablespoons
BROWN 'N SERVE DINNER ROLLS	24 1-ounce rolls

Procedure

1. Combine sugar, lemon rind and juice and butter.

2. Make 3 slits, diagonally across top of each roll, being careful not to cut through bottom crust.

3. Insert about 1/2 teaspoon lemon mixture into each slit in the rolls. Spread any remaining mixture over top of rolls.

4. Place rolls on a shallow baking pan. Bake in oven at 400°F. for 10 to 12 minutes or until golden brown.

BUTTERSCOTCH MUFFINS

Yield: 24 halves

Ingredients

BUTTER or MARGARINE, soft	4 ounces
SUGAR, LIGHT BROWN	12 ounces
PECANS, finely chopped	1 cup
ENGLISH MUFFINS	12

Procedure
1. Combine butter and brown sugar, blending well. Add pecans.
2. Gently pull muffins apart with fingers or fork. Toast lightly.
3. Spread with butter mixture.
4. Place under broiler to finish browning.

TOASTED LEMONADE GINGER MUFFINS

Yield: 48 portions

Ingredients

ENGLISH MUFFINS, large	48
LEMONADE CONCENTRATE, frozen	2 6-ounce cans (1-1/2 cups)
BUTTER or MARGARINE	11 ounces (1-1/3 cups)
GINGER, GROUND	4 teaspoons

Procedure
1. Tear or cut muffins to split horizontally. Place 24 halves on each of 4 bun pans (18-inch by 26-inch by 1-inch), cut side up.
2. Melt lemonade and butter together in a small saucepan; add ginger.
3. Brush muffin halves with butter mixture allowing about 1-1/2 teaspoons per half.
4. Toast in oven at 400°F. for 15 minutes. Serve hot.

Toppings · Fillings · Glazes

BUTTER CRUMB TOPPING

Yield: approximately 6-1/2 pounds

Ingredients

SUGAR, BROWN	12 ounces
SUGAR, GRANULATED	12 ounces
BUTTER	1 pound
SHORTENING	12 ounces
SALT	1/4 ounce
VANILLA	1/4 ounce
EGG YOLKS	3 ounces
FLOUR, BREAD	1-1/2 pounds
FLOUR, CAKE	1-1/2 pounds

Procedure

   1. Cream sugars, butter, shortening, salt, vanilla and egg yolks together until smooth.

   2. Sift bread and cake flour together. Add to creamed mixture; mix by hand only until well-blended.

White and Peach Topping for Danish

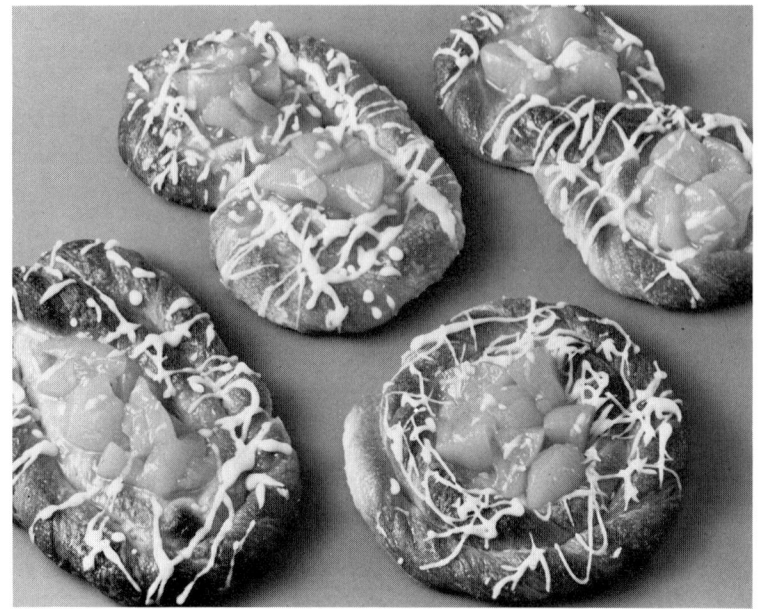

Cling Peach Advisory Board

APPLE-RAISIN FILLING

Yield: 3 cups (for 48 3-inch rolls)

Ingredients

RAISINS, LIGHT or DARK	2 cups
APPLES, GROUND	2 cups
SUGAR	1/2 cup
FLOUR, ALL-PURPOSE	2 tablespoons
LEMON RIND and JUICE from	1/2 lemon
SALT	1/8 teaspoon
WATER	1/2 cup

Procedure

1. Rinse and dry raisins; grind or chop coarsely. Mix all ingredients. Bring to boil; cook 5 minutes, stirring often. Cool.

SIMPLE GLAZE
(For Danish Pastry)

Ingredients
SUGAR	2 pounds
GLUCOSE	2 pounds
WATER	1 quart

Procedure

1. Combine ingredients; bring to a boil. Cool before using to glaze baked Danish pastries.

APRICOT GLAZE

Yield: approximately 5 quarts

Ingredients
APRICOTS	1 No. 10 can
SUGAR	6 pounds
CORN SYRUP, LIGHT	2 pounds

Procedure

1. Rub apricots through a sieve.
2. Add sugar. Bring slowly to a boil; boil for about 5 minutes. Stir in corn syrup. Remove from heat.
3. Use warm or hot, applying with a brush. (Glaze may be stored. Reheat before using.)

POWDERED SUGAR DANISH ICING

Yield: 12-3/4 pounds

Ingredients
SUGAR 6X (CONFECTIONERS')	10 pounds
CORN SYRUP, LIGHT	1-1/4 pounds
VANILLA	1 tablespoon
WATER (approximate amount)	1-1/2 pounds

Procedure

1. Combine ingredients; mix. (Adjust water for consistency.) Keep icing lukewarm for economy and ease of use.

PEACH FILLING FOR DANISH PASTRY

Yield: 2-1/2 quarts

Ingredients

PEACHES, CLING, sliced	1 No. 10 can
CORNSTARCH	1/2 cup
SUGAR	1 cup
SALT	1/2 teaspoon
ALMOND EXTRACT	1 teaspoon
LEMON JUICE	1 tablespoon
YELLOW FOOD COLOR	few drops

Procedure

    1. Drain peaches, saving syrup.

    2. Mix cornstarch, sugar and salt in heavy saucepan. Gradually blend in peach syrup. Cook and stir until mixture is thickened and clear.

    3. Remove from heat. Add almond extract, lemon juice and food color.

    4. Dice peach slices into thickened syrup. Cool.

FILBERT FILLING FOR DANISH PASTRY

Yield: 7 pounds, 6 ounces

Ingredients

FILBERTS, GROUND, roasted	1 pound
SUGAR	2 pounds
CINNAMON	1/2 ounce
EGGS, WHOLE	6 ounces
CAKE CRUMBS	3 pounds
NONFAT DRY MILK	2 ounces
WATER	14 ounces

Procedure

    1. Combine ingredients; mix to a smooth spreading paste.

CHEESE FILLING FOR DANISH PASTRY

Yield: 9-1/2 pounds

Ingredients

COTTAGE CHEESE, BAKERS'	5 pounds
SUGAR	2-1/2 pounds
NONFAT DRY MILK	10 ounces
POWDERED LEMON JUICE	1 ounce
FLOUR	5 ounces
SHORTENING	10 ounces
SALT	1 tablespoon
EGGS, WHOLE	6 ounces (3/4 cup)
VANILLA	as needed

Procedure

1. Place cheese, sugar, nonfat dry milk powder, lemon juice, flour, shortening and salt in mixer bowl; mix smooth.
2. Add eggs gradually; mix smooth.
3. Add vanilla to taste.

Variations

Add 8 ounces currants or chopped raisins. Or, add 1 pound chopped drained pineapple.

ORANGE-ALMOND COFFEE CAKE FILLING

Yield: 2 pounds

Ingredients

NATURAL ALMOND PASTE	1 pound, 8 ounces
EGG, beaten	1 large
SUGAR	2 ounces
ORANGE RIND, grated	1 tablespoon
ORANGE JUICE	1 cup
SALT	1 teaspoon
ALMOND EXTRACT	1 teaspoon

Procedure

1. Break up almond paste.
2. Add remaining ingredients; blend together well.

ALMOND PASTE FILLING FOR COFFEE CAKES

Yield: 2-1/4 pounds

Ingredients

NATURAL ALMOND PASTE	1 pound
EGGS, beaten	1 cup
SUGAR	7 ounces
BUTTER, melted	4 ounces
CAKE CRUMBS, FINE DRY*	2 cups
SALT	1 teaspoon
LEMON RIND, grated	2 teaspoons
LEMON JUICE	1/4 cup

Procedure
1. Break up almond paste.
2. Add remaining ingredients; mix until smooth.

*Increase cake crumbs if less moist filling is desired.

GOLDEN DATE DANISH PASTRIES

Yield: filling for 12 dozen (3-inch) pastries

Ingredients

DATES, pitted	4 pounds
ORANGE JUICE	1-1/2 quarts
LEMON RIND, grated	1 tablespoon
LEMON JUICE	1-1/2 cups
SALT	1-1/2 teaspoons
BUTTER or MARGARINE	3/4 cup (6 ounces)
DANISH PASTRY DOUGH	as needed

Procedure
1. Cut or chop dates into small pieces.
2. Combine dates, orange juice, lemon rind, lemon juice, salt and butter. Cook and stir until thickened, about 5 minutes. Cool.
3. Roll Danish pastry dough thin. Cut into 3-inch squares.
4. Place 1 tablespoon filling in center of each square. Bring corners to center over filling. Turn points back slightly to show filling.
5. Bake in oven at 400°F. until golden brown, about 15 minutes.

DANISH COFFEE CAKE FILLING

Yield: 2-1/2 pounds

Ingredients
NATURAL ALMOND PASTE	2 pounds
EGGS, slightly beaten	1 cup
SALT	1 teaspoon
ALMOND EXTRACT	1 teaspoon
LEMON JUICE	3 tablespoons

Procedure
1. Break up almond paste.
2. Add remaining ingredients; blend together well.

PRUNE FILLING

Yield: approximately 6-3/4 cups

Ingredients
PRUNES, cooked, finely chopped	1-1/2 quarts
SUGAR	1-1/2 cups
CINNAMON	1 tablespoon
CLOVES, GROUND	1-1/2 teaspoons

Procedure
1. Combine ingredients, mixing well.

Pineapple and Peanut Butter Sandwich *(See recipe, p. 234)*

Pineapple Growers Assn.

BREAKFAST AND BRUNCH SANDWICHES

THE PREVAILING TASTE for sandwiches is another enthusiasm that can easily make headway within the breakfast scheme. It's an idea that makes sense. Breakfast sandwiches are easy to put together, quickly served and eaten. Made with toast, ham, bacon, eggs, and similar ingredients, they represent familiar breakfast items in a fresh new guise. Perhaps there <u>has</u> been too much serving of the same old foods in the same old way. Perhaps menus <u>have</u> become too limited, the choices too few.

Pick-up-and-eat sandwiches like a scrambled egg and crumbled bacon on toast or Canadian bacon on toasted sandwich buns should find a wide audience. For other likely suggestions, try offering a toasted sandwich with a cream cheese and ground ham filling; a cream cheese sandwich on toasted raisin bread; a toasted sandwich filled with cream cheese and smoked cheese combined in a tasty blend.

There are other types of sandwiches suited to the breakfast menu and still others, more elaborate, that qualify for brunch. Some are on the moist side so eating calls for a fork. In addition to the recipes that follow, the list could include these:

Crisp bacon strips sandwiched between slices of French toast with a jug of maple syrup served on the side

A French toasted cheese (blend of cottage and cream cheese) sandwich topped with a bright dab of jelly or with strawberry sauce

An open-face scrambled egg sandwich made on toasted halves of an English muffin and topped with sauteed sliced mushrooms and slices of crisp bacon

BAKED TURKEY AND ASPARAGUS SANDWICH AU GRATIN

Yield: 15 sandwiches

Ingredients

TOAST SLICES	30
TURKEY ROLL, thinly sliced	2 pounds
ASPARAGUS SPEARS, cooked	60 large
CREAM OF CHICKEN SOUP, CONDENSED	1 50-ounce can
MILK	1-1/2 cups
WORCESTERSHIRE SAUCE	1 tablespoon
CHEESE, SHARP, shredded	1/2 pound
PIMIENTO STRIPS	as needed

Procedure

1. Cut half the toast slices across forming two triangles. In individual baking dish, place 1 slice toast in center, a toast triangle at each side.

2. Place 2 ounces turkey on each sandwich. Top with 4 spears asparagus.

3. Blend soup, milk and Worcestershire sauce.

4. Ladle 4 ounces soup mixture over each sandwich. Sprinkle with about 2 tablespoons cheese. Garnish with strips of pimiento.

5. Bake in oven at 450°F. for about 10 minutes or until sauce is bubbling and cheese is lightly browned.

EGG SANDWICH AU GRATIN

Yield: 48 sandwiches

Ingredients

TOAST	48 slices
EGGS, hard-cooked, sliced	4 dozen
CHEESE, PROCESS AMERICAN, sliced	48 slices (3 pounds)
CREAM OF CELERY SOUP, CONDENSED	2 51-ounce cans
PIMIENTOS, chopped	1 cup

Procedure

   1. Place toast on baking sheets or in individual baking dishes. Arrange one egg, sliced, on each slice of toast. Top with a slice of cheese.

   2. Combine soup and pimientos; spoon 1/4 cup sauce over each sandwich.

   3. Bake in oven at 375°F. for 20 minutes or until bubbly and hot.

PINEAPPLE FRENCH TOAST SANDWICH

Yield: 50 sandwiches

Ingredients

CREAM CHEESE	2 pounds
CRUSHED PINEAPPLE, drained	1 quart
SALT	1 teaspoon
RAISIN BREAD	100 slices
EGGS, slightly beaten	1 quart (2 pounds)
MILK	1 quart
SALT	1 tablespoon

Procedure

   1. Combine cream cheese, pineapple and first amount of salt. Spread a No. 30 scoop of filling on half the slices of bread. Cover with remaining slices.

   2. Combine eggs, milk and remaining salt.

   3. Dip sandwiches in egg mixture until well coated. Cook on well-greased griddle, turning to brown both sides.

   4. Serve hot with maple syrup.

FRENCH TOASTED MUSHROOM SANDWICH

Yield: 24

Ingredients

BUTTER or MARGARINE	6 ounces
SALT	1/4 teaspoon
MUSHROOMS, FRESH, chopped	1-1/4 gallons (4 pounds, as purchased)
ENRICHED BREAD SLICES	48
EGGS, whole	1-1/3 cups
MILK, SKIM	2-2/3 cups
SALT	2 teaspoons
PEPPER	1/4 teaspoon

Procedure

1. Melt half of the butter in each of two large aluminum or stainless steel skillets.

2. Add 1/8 teaspoon salt and 2-1/2 quarts chopped mushrooms to each skillet; saute until done over medium heat.

3. Make sandwiches using a No. 16 scoop of mushroom filling between two bread slices.

4. Beat eggs, milk, remaining salt and pepper together.

5. Dip sandwiches in egg mixture coating both sides. Grill on a lightly-greased griddle.

CHICKEN-MUSHROOM SOUFFLE SANDWICH

Yield: 45 portions

Ingredients

ENRICHED BREAD, FRESH or DAY-OLD	90 slices
BUTTER or MARGARINE, soft	5-1/4 ounces
CHICKEN, cooked and sliced or chopped	2 pounds, 14 ounces
CREAM OF MUSHROOM SOUP, CONDENSED	1-1/2 51-ounce cans
MILK	2 quarts
TARRAGON, crushed	1-1/2 teaspoons
PARMESAN CHEESE, grated	4 ounces
BACON, slices	45
MUSHROOM CAPS, small	3 pounds

Procedure

1. Trim crusts from bread. Spread slices with butter.
2. Using chicken as filling, make each 2 slices of bread into a sandwich. Lay 15 sandwiches flat on the bottom of each of 3 greased 12-inch by 20-inch by 2-1/2 inch steam table pans, fitting them close together.
3. Combine soup, milk and tarragon. Pour over sandwiches allowing 1/3 of the mixture to each pan. Sprinkle cheese evenly over sandwiches.
4. Bake in oven at 450°F. for 20 minutes, or until browned.
5. Cut bacon slices in half, crosswise; fry or broil until crisp.
6. Saute mushrooms in bacon drippings.
7. Serve sandwiches garnished with bacon and mushrooms.

PINEAPPLE AND PEANUT BUTTER SANDWICH
(See picture, p. 228)

Yield: 25 portions, 1 No. 30 scoop filling per portion

Ingredients

PEANUT BUTTER	1-1/2 pounds
PINEAPPLE, CRUSHED, drained	1 No. 2 can (2-1/2 cups, undrained)
BUTTER, softened	1/4 pound
WHITE BREAD	50 slices
EGGS, beaten	12
MILK	1-1/2 cups
BANANAS, RIPE	5
*PINEAPPLE SAUCE	6-1/4 cups

Procedure

1. Combine peanut butter, drained crushed pineapple and butter. Spread a No. 30 scoop of filling on each of 25 slices of bread. Cover with remaining bread slices.

2. Combine eggs and milk. Dip sandwiches into mixture. Fry on lightly-greased griddle, turning to brown on both sides.

3. Garnish with banana slices. Serve hot with pineapple sauce.

*PINEAPPLE SAUCE

Yield: approximately 2 quarts

Ingredients

PINEAPPLE JUICE	1 46-ounce can
SUGAR	1 cup
CORNSTARCH	6 tablespoons
SALT	1/2 teaspoon
PINEAPPLE, CRUSHED	1 No. 2 can (2-1/2 cups)
LEMON JUICE	1 tablespoon

Procedure

1. Heat pineapple juice.

2. Mix sugar, cornstarch and salt; add gradually to hot juice. Bring slowly to a boil, stirring constantly. Cook until clear.

3. Add crushed pineapple and lemon juice; reheat to boiling point. Serve hot.

BROILED MUSHROOM CHEESEWICH

Yield: 12

Ingredients

CREAM OF MUSHROOM SOUP, undiluted	2-1/2 cups
CHEESE, CHEDDAR, shredded	12 ounces
EGGS, slightly beaten	2
LIQUID HOT PEPPER SEASONING	1/4 teaspoon
BREAD	12 slices
TOMATO SLICES	12
SALT	as needed

Procedure

1. Combine soup, cheese, eggs and pepper seasoning; mix well.
2. Toast one side of bread under broiler. Spread filling over untoasted side.
3. Top with tomato slice; sprinkle with salt.
4. Broil until cheese melts and filling is bubbly.

TOASTED TURKEY SANDWICH

Yield: 24 sandwiches

Ingredients

BACON STRIPS	12 (3/4 pound)
BUTTER or MARGARINE, soft	1/4 pound
ENRICHED BREAD SLICES, toasted	48
TURKEY, cooked, 1-1/2 ounce slices	24 (2-1/4 pounds)

Procedure

1. Cook bacon until crisp; crumble into soft butter; blend thoroughly.
2. For each sandwich: lightly spread 2 slices of hot toast with bacon butter, allowing 1/2 teaspoon for each slice. Fill with 1-1/2 ounces sliced turkey. Serve immediately.

GRILLED BACON AND EGG SANDWICH →

Yield: 24 sandwiches (1 egg, 2 slices bread, 1 bacon strip)

Ingredients

ENRICHED BREAD	48 slices
BUTTER or MARGARINE, soft	4 ounces
EGGS, hard-cooked	24
SALT	2-1/2 teaspoons
PEPPER	1/8 teaspoon
BACON SLICES	24 (1-1/2 pounds)

BROILED CHEESE AND FRUIT SANDWICH

Yield: 50 portions

Ingredients

PRUNES, plumped, chopped	1-1/2 quarts
LEMON JUICE	1 tablespoon
ALLSPICE	1/2 teaspoon
SALAD DRESSING	1/2 cup
BREAD, buttered	50 slices
CHEESE, PROCESS SWISS or AMERICAN	50 slices
BREAD, toasted	50 slices
BACON, broiled	50 slices

Procedure

    1. Combine prunes, lemon juice, allspice and salad dressing.

    2. Place a No. 30 scoop of prune mixture on buttered bread. Spread evenly. Cover with a slice of cheese.

    3. Broil until cheese begins to melt and crusts are browned.

    4. Arrange broiled sandwich in center of serving plate.

    5. Cut toast diagonally; arrange on each side of sandwich. Garnish with bacon. Serve hot.

Procedure

1. Lightly butter each slice of bread.
2. Arrange a sliced hard-cooked egg on each of 24 buttered bread slices. Sprinkle with salt and pepper. Cover with remaining bread, placing buttered side down.
3. Top each sandwich with 2 half slices of bacon.
4. Toast or grill sandwiches, as ordered.

On griddle or broiler: cook with bacon side up first. Turn; cook on other side.

In closed grill: toast at 400°F. until bacon is done and sandwich is toasted.

HOT CHICKEN GIBLET SANDWICH

Yield: 25 sandwiches

Ingredients

CHICKEN GIZZARDS and HEARTS (uncooked)	6-1/2 pounds
CHICKEN LIVERS	2 pounds
SALT	1 tablespoon
CHICKEN GRAVY	3 quarts
BREAD SLICES	50
WHIPPED POTATOES	25 4-ounce portions

Procedure

1. Place gizzards and hearts in one flat pan, chicken livers in another. Sprinkle with salt. Steam until tender. Allow 30 minutes for livers, longer for hearts and gizzards.
2. Drain in colander; rinse well.
3. Cut gizzards into 4 pieces each.
4. Add all giblets to chicken gravy.
5. Trim crusts from bread if desired. Allow 2 slices per sandwich. Cut one slice across diagonally. Arrange triangles either side of whole slice on plate. Place a portion of whipped potatoes beside bread; 6 ounces giblet and gizzard gravy on bread and potatoes.
6. Garnish with parsley and a souffle cup of cranberry relish.

238 BREAKFAST AND BRUNCH DISHES

Breakfast Sandwich Features Chicken Square

Pillsbury Food Service

COUNTRY SQUIRE SANDWICH

Yield: 20 sandwiches

Ingredients

VIENNA BREAD	2 1-pound loaves
ASPARAGUS SPEARS, cooked	80 (4 to 5 pounds)
HAM, BOILED, 1-ounce slices	20 slices
PROCESS SWISS CHEESE, 1-ounce slices	20 slices

Procedure

    1. Cut each loaf of bread diagonally into 10 1-inch slices.

    2. Wrap 4 asparagus spears in each slice of ham; place on bread slices.

    3. Cut cheese slices in half, diagonally. Cover each ham and asparagus sandwich with two overlapping triangles of cheese.

    4. Bake or broil to order. Place on baking sheet; bake in oven at 400°F. or broil under low heat for 5 minutes, or until cheese melts.

FRENCHED CHERRY-CHEESE SANDWICH

Yield: 50 portions

Ingredients

CHEESE, PROCESS, shredded	3 pounds
MARASCHINO CHERRIES, chopped	1 quart
RAISINS, chopped	1 pound
DATES, chopped	1 pound
MAYONNAISE	3 cups
BREAD	100 slices
EGGS, beaten	24
MILK	1-1/2 quarts
SALT	1 teaspoon

Procedure

    1. Combine cheese, cherries, raisins, dates and mayonnaise.

    2. Spread on half of the bread slices. Top with remaining slices.

    3. Combine eggs, milk and salt.

    4. Dip sandwiches in egg mixture; brown on both sides on griddle or grill.

DEVONSHIRE SANDWICH

Yield: 50 sandwiches

Ingredients

TOAST	50 slices
BREAST OF CHICKEN, cooked, sliced	6 pounds
TOMATO SLICES	50
BACON, cooked	50 slices
CREAM OF CHICKEN or MUSHROOM SOUP	3 51-ounce cans
CHEESE, AMERICAN, grated	1 pound

Procedure

   1. Arrange toast in individual shallow baking dishes. Top with chicken, tomato slices and bacon.
   2. Combine soup and cheese in saucepan. Heat and stir until cheese melts.
   3. Pour approximately 1/3 cup sauce over each sandwich.
   4. Broil until sauce bubbles and is lightly browned.

EGG-BACON SANDWICH FILLING

Yield: 1 gallon (Makes 48 sandwiches using No. 12 scoop filling)

Ingredients

EGGS, hard-cooked, chopped	1 gallon (5 pounds, 6 ounces)
BACON, cooked, finely chopped	2-1/2 quarts (5 pounds raw bacon)
MAYONNAISE or SALAD DRESSING	1 quart

Procedure

   1. Combine ingredients, mixing well.

FRENCH TOASTED COTTAGE CHEESE SANDWICH

Yield: 24 sandwiches

Ingredients

COTTAGE CHEESE	3 pounds
ALMONDS, diced, roasted (optional)	1 cup
MAYONNAISE	1 cup
RAISIN BREAD	48 slices
EGGS, beaten	6
MILK	3 cups
SALT	1/4 teaspoon
ORANGE MARMALADE	2 cups

Procedure

1. Combine cottage cheese, almonds and mayonnaise.
2. Make sandwiches with raisin bread using No. 20 scoop of mixture for each sandwich.
3. Combine beaten eggs, milk and salt.
4. Dip sandwiches quickly into milk mixture to coat both sides.
5. Cook on hot buttered grill, turning once, until golden on both sides.
6. Serve hot with marmalade.

Elegance Frames Brunch Buffet Specialties

National Live Stock and Meat Board

BREAKFAST BUFFETS

THE BREAKFAST BUFFET is flexible. Interpret it as you will. It offers advantages for catering special functions. It also holds attractive potential for expediting service, for dramatizing a menu, and giving a mark of individuality to your regular breakfast hour. Over all, a well-planned buffet service can lessen the labor load, help speed up service and make your breakfast or brunch a more attractive meal.

Your buffet can range from a very simple presentation to a full-fledged display of dishes, hot and cold. By featuring a table d'hote menu where everyone takes the same thing, you can serve sizable special groups quickly and yet graciously with a minimum of help. Such a scheme will take on added charm when you do something excitingly different in the way you present the food.

For greatest success, be sure to create the impression of "plenty." Make a point of using colorful accessories, think up attractive garnishes and provide other imaginative extras to create a festive, party-like mood.

When planning the menu for a breakfast function, experiment with new ideas. Try a fruit with a newsworthy note, in-

troduce something special in the way of bread, add a choice of preserves with unusual appeal. But when it comes to hot foods, limit yourself to items that can be ready in sufficient quantity to serve at the time they are needed. These should also be items that can stand up through the holding period that may be required. Oven-prepared dishes are a boon when large amounts are needed for a crowd. Items such as a corned beef hash bake, oven-browned ham and pineapple kebabs, country sausage and apple rings, a risotto with chicken livers and mushrooms, ham with carrot and pineapple sauce, baked eggs in bacon rings and oven-baked pancakes with sausages and apricot sauce are sure to go over well.

How you apply the buffet system to your regular (or daily) breakfast service depends on the particular dictates of your own situation. In general, people's breakfast eating habits tend to follow one of two patterns. Some want a small or Continental-type breakfast of coffee with some form of bread, plus juice or fruit. Others prefer a larger meal rounded out with an addition of hot or cold cereal and/or an egg dish, bacon, sausages, or some other breakfast dish of the heartier sort. There are a number of different arrangements that can meet everyone's needs.

One of the simplest buffets consists exclusively of a tempting array of fruits and juices, available either to fill an order given to the waiter or to invite patrons to serve themselves. (When presenting juices in large pitchers, remember to have a long-handled stirring spoon at hand.) With this small-scale buffet arrangement the remainder of the meal is served from the kitchen in the conventional way.

For a little more elaborate buffet table—but one still confined to cold foods—add an assortment of ready-to-eat cereals in large matching glass bowls and a display of plain and sweet rolls or other breakfast breads. Plus, if desired, a selection of likely cheeses and sliced cold meats. Make eggs, toast, and other hot dishes available on order.

A more inclusive buffet equipped to serve hot foods as well as cold can be arranged as one long table or in two parallel set-ups, one section for the basic small meal and the other with hot dish to be added. This can be easily handled by offering two fixed-price menus, the higher tab applying when a hot, entree-type dish is chosen. Be sure to keep the hot dishes hot, adding freshly heated foods as needed.

A buffet of this complete scope allows for a visual display that will merchandise your food far more successfully than any written menu. The plan also keeps the waitresses within the serving area, ready to re-set tables, circulate with coffee, and fill in the amount of the breakfast checks.

On any buffet, fruits adding a splash of color can easily carry off honors as the most eye-catching portion of your entire display. On-premise baked specialties like kuchens, muffins and freshly made doughnuts can make a tremendous hit. But it is, after all, the hot food that offers the greatest latitude for original expression. Extra touches can lure patrons to try the larger menu pattern. It's the area where, at breakfast or brunch, you can promote house specialties, feature regional cuisine, and use showmanship to stir fresh interest in dishes that have been favorites for years.

Explore the things that you can do with chicken livers, Canadian bacon, creamed chipped beef and fish. Don't fail to take advantage of the ways you can employ vegetables like mushrooms, tomatoes, asparagus, potatoes and spinach. Or, the many fascinating dishes you can prepare with eggs.

For a bit of drama, set up an omelet bar with all the makings and a variety of fillings and offer custom-made omelets to suit the patrons' whims. Or, offer soft, creamy scrambled eggs with a selection of toppings which might be taken from a list such as this:

Diced fresh tomato	Parmesan cheese
Sour cream and chives	Roasted chopped almonds
Sauteed chopped mushrooms	Cottage cheese
Crumbled bacon	Snipped dried beef
Chopped parsley	

REGIONAL BUFFET MENUS

An excellent way to capture breakfast or brunch buffet interest is to feature regional buffet menus. They can also bring in group breakfast business. Choose one of the regional menus on the following pages for a special occasion. These menus can also be scheduled on a weekly basis to build business on a low volume day.

Buffet Service for Continental Breakfast

Pillsbury Co.

Eggs Benedict on a Brunch Buffet

National Live Stock and Meat Board

Breakfast Buffets 247

Spanish Scramble with Cherryam Muffins

Spanish Green Olive Commission and Louisiana Yam Commission

Meat Styled for Brunch

National Live Stock and Meat Board

NEW ENGLAND

Chilled cranberry juice
Warm baked apples
Blueberries with cream and maple sugar

Codfish cakes with tomato sauce
Boston baked beans and brown bread
Red flannel hash
Creamed cod and eggs on toast points
Fried corn meal mush with maple syrup
Blueberry griddle cakes with sausage patties

Hot Johnnie cake
Graham muffins
Cranberry kuchen
Blueberry muffins

Apple pie
Soft molasses cookies
Sugared doughnuts

PENNSYLVANIA DUTCH

Scrapple with glazed apple rings
Ham, bacon or sausage with home-fried potatoes
Potato pancakes with fresh applesauce
Creamed chipped beef
Dried corn pudding
Fruit fritters with syrup
Cottage cheese with apple butter
Cinnamon buns
Funnel cakes
Fastnachts (yeast-raised doughnuts)
Streusel coffee cake
Crumb cookies
Funny cake
Shoo-fly pie

MIDWESTERN

Chilled apple juice
Sliced fresh peaches
Huckleberries and cream
Cinnamon applesauce

Ready-to-eat cereals with cream

Fried eggs with crisp bacon strips and hash brown potatoes
Chicken hash
Pork chops
Fluffy wheat cakes with maple syrup

Bran muffins
Frosted coffee cake
Toasted cinnamon rolls
Jelly doughnuts

SOUTHERN

Fresh figs with cream
Sliced peaches
Sugared fresh strawberries
Assorted melon balls

Ham with red-eye gravy
Crab cakes
Sauteed shrimp with hominy
Poached eggs with grits
Spoonbread with scrambled calves brains
Pecan waffles with cane syrup

Crusty Southern corn muffins
Scones
Corn bread sticks
Cracklin' bread
Sally Lunn
Crusty biscuits (small, thin and piping hot)

250   BREAKFAST AND BRUNCH DISHES

WESTERN

*Sliced oranges
Red raspberries with cream
Cranshaw melon wedges
Cantaloupe brushed with honey
Ripe papaya halves*

*Brook trout saute with almonds
Baked hash topped with peaches
Fluffy French toast with pineapple sauce*

*Hot biscuits with syrup
Raisin bread toast
Date muffins*

Finale with a Flourish

Pillsbury Co.

Crepes filled with tangy berry sauce and topped with whole fruit provide a memorable ending for a leisurely brunch.

CHOLESTEROL AND THE BREAKFAST MENU

OPERATORS WISHING to make a menu provision for patrons who have cholesterol content in mind should remember that recommended foods include:

- Fruits
- Bread and cereal products
- Margarine (kinds that place vegetable oils first on the ingredient list)
- Vegetable oils
- Skim milk
- Plain yoghurt
- Fish
- Poultry (without skin)
- Frozen cholesterol-free egg substitute
- Lean meats
- Uncreamed cottage cheese
- Nuts
- Peanut butter
- Vegetables

Fruit, bread and cereals are naturals for the breakfast menu. Here are some suggested items with a higher protein content:

No-Cholesterol Challah, Muffins, Spoon Bread

Standard Brands, Inc.

A fruit plate of melon crescents (or other large pieces of fruit) arranged with a scoop of uncreamed cottage cheese topped with slivered almonds

Fingers of cold chicken or turkey arranged with whole strawberries, sliced oranges and pineapple chunks

Chilled fruit soup topped with uncreamed cottage cheese and a sprinkling of toasted slivered almonds

Scrambled eggs, French toast and omelets prepared with frozen cholesterol-free egg substitute (Omelet with mushrooms, parsley, tomatoes or jelly)

French toasted peanut butter sandwich (prepared with the cholesterol-free egg substitute) topped with sliced bananas and pineapple sauce

A small whole brook trout sauteed in vegetable oil and garnished with almonds

INDEX

Beverages 7-9
  See Fruits, Juices, Beverages
BREADS, Introduction 122-24
  Biscuits, Biscuit Sweet
    Rolls: 177-78
    Recipes 178-82
      Apple Roll-Ups 180
      Apple Sauce Pinwheels,
        Quick 181
      Baking Powder
        Biscuits 178
      Iced Date Biscuit Rolls 179
      Maple Raisin Twists 182
      Orange Pinwheels 180-81
  Coffee Cakes: 154
    Recipes 155-69
      Apple 165
        Dutch 169
        Rolled Oats 166
      Breakfast 164-65
      Caramel Date 164
      Cherry Raisin 160
      Cinnamon Crumb 163
      Cranberry Nut Squares 161
      Graham-Nut 156
      Hawaiian Breakfast 162
      Honey
        Crisp 159
        Nut 155
      Mincemeat 168
      Orange 157
      Raisin 158
  Corn Bread: 148
    Recipes 149-53
      Corn Hominy Sticks 151
      Pineapple 150
      Sesame Cheese 152
      Southern 152
      Spoonbread 150-51
      Sticks 149
      Sweet Potato Pone 153
  Doughnuts: 200-02
    Recipes 203-11
      Cinnamon-Pecan,
        Toasted 208
      Crullers, Louisiana 207
      Honey Glaze 208
      Lemon-Coconut 209
      Maple-Nut 209
      Praline 204
        Icing 205

Sherry Puff Balls,
  Sherry Glaze 203
Spiced 210-11
White Frosting 205
Yeast-Raised, Tasty
  Rich 206
Kuchen: 194-95
  Recipes 196-99
    Blueberry or Apple 199
    Cranberry 196
    Prune-Orange, Quick 197
Muffins: 125
  Recipes 126-47
    Almond, Jelly Topped 140
    Apple-Nut 127
    Basic 126
    Blueberry 128-29
    Bran 138
      Basic Whole Bran
        Mix 140-41
      Peanut Butter 136
      Whole 139
      With Crunchy
        Topping 146
    Branana 137
    Caraway Cheese 136-37
    Cherry 144
    Corn 134
    Cranberry-Orange 147
    Filbert Nut,
      Old-Fashioned 135
    Gingerbread 131
    Golden Corn 128
    Graham 132
    Mincemeat 132
    Peanut Butter
      Apple 133
      Bran 136
    Pecan
      Gems 144-45
      Whole Wheat 142
    Pineapple Upside-down
      Ginger 130
    Prune 145
    Pumpkin 141
    Raisin Peanut Filling 129
    Yam-Nut 143
Quick Loaf: 170-72
  Recipes 172-76
    Banana Tea or
      Muffins 174-75

254 BREAKFAST AND BRUNCH DISHES

Boston Brown	175
Butterscotch Raisin	174
Nut	172
Spiced Butter-	
scotch	176
Prune	173
Yeast Rolls:	183
Recipes	184-93
Cheese	187
Cherry-Filled Breakfast	
Bread	189
Cinnamon Twist	185
Danish Pastry,	
Average Richness	191
Rich	192
Sweet Roll Mix	193
Oatmeal, Raised	186-87
Orange, Glazed	184
Parisienne Brioches	188
Raisin Cheese Buns	186
Sweet Rolls, Filled	190
Breakfast	3-5
Breakfast and Brunch Sand-	
wiches	228-30
Recipes	230-41
Bacon Egg, Grilled	236-37
Baked Turkey and	
Asparagus au Gratin	230
Cheese and Fruit Sand-	
wiches, Broiled	236
Chicken Giblet	237
Chicken Mushroom	
Souffle	233
Country Squire Sandwich	239
Devonshire Sandwich	240
Egg and Bacon Sandwich	
Filling	240
Egg au Gratin	231
French Toasted Cottage	
Cheese Sandwich	241
French Toasted Mushroom	
Sandwich	232
Frenched Cherry-Cheese	
Sandwich	239
Mushroom Cheesewich,	
Broiled	235
Pineapple and Peanut	
Butter	234
Pineapple French Toast	231
Pineapple Sauce	234
Turkey, Toasted	235
Breakfast Buffets	242-50
Regional Menus	
Midwestern	249
New England	248
Pennsylvania Dutch	248
Southern	249
Western	250
Butter, *see Syrups*	
Cereals	18-21
Recipes	22-25
Baked Grits	22
Broiled Peach Slices with	
Crunch Topping	23
Rice	
Croquettes with Hot	
Spiced Applesauce	24
Scalloped	23
Chicken, *see Meat, Chicken and Fish*	
Cholesterol and the Breakfast	
Menu	251-52
Egg Dishes	90-91
Recipes	92-103
Benedict	96, 98
Casserole of Baked	
Spinach	94
Croquettes and Celery	
Sauce	100
Florentine	95
Gourmet Scramble	98
Quiche, Fresh Mushroom	99
Scrambled	101
Herb	102
Oven with Cheese	103
Sherry Hollandaise Sauce	97
Shirred Bretonne	94-95
Tomato-Egg Scramble	92
Village Ham 'N Eggs	93
See also Omelets	
Fillings, *see Toppings, Fillings, Glazes, etc.*	
Fish, *see Meat, Chicken and Fish*	
French Toast	76-78
Recipes	79-83
Cinnamon-Nut	81
Cinnamon Orange	79
Deep Fried	79
Deviled Ham	82
Fluffy Parmesan	80
Grilled Custard	82
Oven	80-81
With Strawberry Butter	83
Fritters	71
Recipes	72-75
Apple	72
Cherry	75
Corn	74
Ham and Corn	73

Index 255

Prune	74-75
Fruits, Juices, Beverages	6-9
Recipes	10-17
Apples	
Hot Buttered	14
Scalloped	10
Banana-Orange Shake	17
Chocolate Banana Milk	
Shake	17
Fruit Cocktail Filling,	
Basic	13
Fruit Compote	15
Spiced Hot	15
Fruits, Hot Spiced	16
Grapefruit, Broiled	
Sherried	11
Honeydew Boats Filled	
with Citrus Sections	10
Kooshab	14
Mocha-Flavored Hot	
Cocoa	17
Peach Filling, Basic	13
Pizza (Color Wheel)	12
3-on-the-Rocks	16
Gingerbread, *see* Scones, Gingerbread, Popovers and Sally Lunn	
Glazes, *see* Toppings, Fillings, Glazes,	
Introduction	1
Juices, *see* Fruits, Juices, Beverages	
Meat, Chicken and Fish	26-27
Recipes	28-51
Apple Rings, Baked	29
Apricot Sauce	30
Chicken Creamed	
Josephine	42
Chicken-Filled Crepes	43
Chicken Liver	
Saute	44
Spaghetti with	38
Codfish Balls	46
Crab-Fish Cakes	47
Creamed Chipped Beef and Eggs en Casserole	40
Fish Patties, Baked	48
Ham	
and Apples, Escalloped	34
and Mushrooms, Creamed	33
and Sweetbreads Florentine	35
Balls in Sour Cream Gravy	36
with Carrot-Pineapple Sauce	33
Hash	
Corned Beef with Peaches	41
Roast Beef	39
Herbed Egg Sauce	49
Liver	
Broiled	44
on Rice	45
Meat Sandwich, Baked	31
Oyster Mushroom Brochette	51
Pineapple Hash Pie	40-41
Potato Salmon Patties	49
Prune Jambalaya	37
Sausage	
Country and Apple Rings	29
In Oven-Baked Pancakes	30
Noodle Casserole	28
Scrapple	32
Sour Cream Gravy	36
Trout	
Coconut-Lemon	51
Seasoned Fresh	50
Omelets	104-06
Recipes	107-13
Filling	106
French	108-09
Hong Kong Sauce	109
Mousseline Dessert	113
Mushroom	112
Plain	107
Sauces	106
Spanish	110-11
Two-Egg	108
Pancakes	52-55
Recipes	55-63
Apple Pancake Stacks	60
Blueberry Griddle	56
Bread Crumb Griddle	57
Brown Sugar Whip	55
Buttermilk Hot Cakes	58-59
Cinnamon Hard Sauce	56
Crepes	60-61
Delicate Thin	62
Gingerbread with Fruited Whipped Cream	59
Ham and Jam	63
Olive Flapjacks with Cheese Sauce	58
Rice	61
Sugar 'N Spice	55
Variations	57

256   BREAKFAST AND BRUNCH DISHES

Popovers, *see Scones, Gingerbread, Popovers and Sally Lunn*	
Potato Dishes	117
Recipes	118-20
Concord	119
Muffets	118
Puff Balls	120
Sweet Potato Balls	119
Sally Lunn, *see Scones, Gingerbread, Popovers and Sally Lunn*	
Sandwiches, *see Breakfast and Brunch Sandwiches*	
Sauces	
Apricot	30
Celery	100
Cinnamon Hard	56
Herbed Egg	49
Omelet Sauce, Hong Kong	109
Pineapple	234
Sherry Hollandaise	97
See also Syrups	
Scones, Gingerbread, Popovers and Sally Lunn	
Recipes	212-16
Gingerbread	215
Popovers	212
Sally Lunn, Quick	216
Scones	
Raisin	213
Yam	214
Shortcakes and Benedict	114
Recipes	115-16
Asparagus Benedict	115
Fresh Tomato Shortcake	115
Plantation Shortcake	116
Special Treatment	217-20
Apple-Cinnamon Toast	218
Butterscotch Muffins	220
Cinnamon-Orange Loaf	218-19
Lemon Rolls	219
Mushroom Milk Toast	217
Toasted Lemonade Ginger Muffins	220
Syrups	84
Recipes	85-89
Apple Syrup Pancake Sauce	88
Browned Sugar Ginger Syrup	85
Brown Sugar Whip	55
Buttered Pineapple Pancake Sauce	87
Cherry Pancake	89
Cinnamon Honey Butter	88
Cranberry	85
Honey, Hot Spiced	88
Orange Honey Butter	89
Spiced Bing Cherry Sauce	86
Spiced Peach and Raisin	87
Strawberry Butter	86
Toppings, Fillings, Glazes, etc.	221-27
Almond Paste for Coffee Cakes	226
Apple Raisin Filling	222
Apricot Glaze	223
Butter-Crumb Topping	221
Cheese for Danish Pastry Filling	225
Danish Coffee Cake Filling	227
Filbert for Danish Pastry Filling	224
Golden Date Danish Pastries	226
Orange-Almond Coffee Cake	225
Peach for Danish Pastry	224
Powdered Sugar Danish Icing	223
Prune Filling	227
Simple Glaze	223
Waffles	64-66
Recipes	67-70
Cherries Jubilee	70
Cinnamon Pear Crested with Cinnamon Syrup	68-69
Filbert	69
Sherried Shrimp on Variations	68
	67
With Red Red Topping	70

DATE DUE